# PAUL CAMBRIA

# Bridging the Reality Gap

## *Understanding and Relating to the Neurotypical World*

*To my four children, Gianluca, Nicholas, Michael and Nebi, who are the light of my life and the source of my joy. You have taught me the meaning of love, patience, and resilience. You have made me proud of your achievements and inspired by your potential. You have filled my days with laughter and warmth. You are my greatest gift and my greatest responsibility.*

# Contents


*Foreword*     vi

*Preface*     viii

*Acknowledgments*     x

I   Part One

1   The Unseen Dimension: Living in Another Reality     3

     Subchapter 1: The Unseen Current: Navigating the Early Storm     6

     Subchapter 2: Finding My Frequency: Rebuilding and Redefining     7

2   The Invisible Burden: Unmasking ADHD and the Weight of...     10

     Section 1: Introduction: Decoding ADHD and its Unseen Challenges     10

     Section 2: Public Perception of ADHD: Bridging the Empathy Gap     17

     Section 3: Coping with Stigma: Strategies for Resilience and Empowerment     20

Section 4: Stories of Americans with ADHD: Voices from the Front Lines of Stigma     24

Section 5: Conclusion: Embracing the Neurodivergent Future     29

3 The Entrepreneurial Superpower: Harnessing ADHD for...     33

Section 2: The ADHD Entrepreneurial Toolkit: Strengths Redefined     36

Section 3: Navigating the Entrepreneurial Minefield: Managing ADHD Pitfalls     41

Section 4: Trailblazers: Inspiring ADHD Entrepreneurs     45

Section 5: Conclusion: Your Entrepreneurial Blueprint     50

II   Part Two

4 The Authentic Heart: Cultivating Connectedness and Emotional...     55

Section 1: Connectedness, Not Just Connection: The Neurodivergent Path to Belonging     55

Section 2: The Emotional Lives of Neurodivergent Adults: Intensity, Authenticity, and Regulation     61

By integrating these strategies, neurodivergent adults can navigate their rich and intense emotional lives with greater skill and self-acceptance, fostering genuine connectedness and a profound sense of well-being, allowing their authentic heart to thrive.     68

5  The Invisible Agony: DDD Parents Facing Divorce, Parental...     69

   Section 1: Validating the Traumatic Nature of Emotional and Systemic Distancing     70

   Section 2: Letting Go by Embracing Harsh Reality: Neuro-Affirming Healing Strategies     75

   Section 3: The Horrors of Neurotypical Ghosting and Its Devastating Effects on DDD Victims     81

6  Mastering the Emotional Symphony: Navigating and...     86

   Section 1: Recognizing and Naming Your Emotions: Tuning into Your Inner Landscape     88

   Section 2: Validating Your Emotions: The Anchor of Acceptance     90

   Section 3: Expressing Your Emotions: Creative Release and Authentic Communication     92

   Section 4: Regulating Your Emotions: Dopaminergic Strategies for Stability     94

Section 5: Transforming Your Emotions: Rewiring the Brain
for Growth     97

Section 6: Recognizing Your "Emotional Children": Healing
Past Wounds     99

Section 7: Becoming the Emotional
Adult: Integration and Empowerment     101

7 Navigating the Neurotypical Emotional
Landscape: DDD Mastery...     105

Section 1: Emotional Self-Regulation:
Harmonizing Your Inner Symphony     107

Section 2: Decoding the Neurotypical Code: Protecting Your
Emotional Sovereignty     114

8 Unseen Repercussions: Understanding
and Adapting...     122

The Neurodivergent Social Landscape: Understanding the
Mismatch     123

Common Unintentional DDD Social
Blunders and Their DDD Roots     124

Leveraging Your DDD Strengths for
Social Flourishing: A Proactive Approach     133

9 Weaving Your Web: Authentic Networking and Finding Your...     137

The Neurodivergent Networking Imperative: Why We Seek Our
Tribe     139

Section 1: Seeking Your People: Curating Your Authentic Network     140

Section 2: Being Ready: Proactive Strategies for Authentic Engagement     144

Section 3: Being Yourself: Embracing Your DDD Identity in Networking     148

10 Conclusion     152

The Paradigm Shift: Reclaiming the Narrative of Dopamine Deficit Disorder     154

The Dual Nature: Strengths and Challenges of the DDD Brain     155

The External Burden: Navigating a World Not Built for DDD     157

The Path to Empowerment: Strategies for Bridging the Gap     160

The Continuum Dopaminergique: A Vision for Neuro-Inclusion     163

A Call to Action: Your Role in Shaping the Future     164

Epilogue     169

The Unfolding Manifesto: Embodying DDD and Co-Creating a Neuro-Inclusive Future     169

Afterword     183

The Echo of Urgency, the Resonance of Identity – Continuing the LexiNeuroHub Journey     183

*About the Author*     188

# Foreword

As someone who has navigated life with **Dopamine Deficit Disorder (DDD)**, I deeply understand the unique challenges of living in a world primarily structured for neurotypical brains. Yet, I also know the profound joy and reward that comes from unearthing and embracing our distinct strengths and inherent gifts. It is this understanding that makes me truly honored to introduce this transformative book, a truly invaluable resource for anyone touched by DDD or eager to deepen their understanding.

*Dopamine Deficit Disorder: A Manifesto of Urgency & Identity* is a groundbreaking work that transcends conventional narratives. It offers profound insights, actionable strategies, and practical wisdom on how to bridge the often-perceived gap between the DDD brain and the neurotypical world. Authored by a neurodivergent voice, this book courageously shares personal stories and perspectives with disarming honesty and resonant humor. Crucially, its foundations are built upon the latest neuroscientific research, expert guidance, and relatable examples from individuals who live with DDD every day.

This book will illuminate your inner landscape, fostering a deeper understanding of yourself and enabling more effective and authentic connections with others. It will empower you to recognize and celebrate your inherent strengths—such as your boundless creativity, your innovative problem-solving abilities, and your unwavering passion—as true advantages. You will discover practical skills and cultivate habits designed to navigate common challenges like **Inattention Modulation Instability (IMA)**, **Volition and Task Organization (VTO)**, and **Phenotype of Urgency for Reward (PUR)**. Furthermore, it offers vital tools for communicating effectively and assertively in all spheres of life, particularly in professional and educational environments. You will learn to cultivate healthy and supportive relationships with family, friends, and romantic partners, finding profound meaning and purpose by fiercely pursuing your authentic passions and goals.

Crucially, this book is not a manual for "fixing" or "changing" your DDD brain. Instead, it is a passionate guide to embracing and appreciating its extraordinary design. It is also an invitation to share your rich stories and unique perspectives with the neurotypical world, fostering mutual learning and understanding. Ultimately, it is a testament to the immense diversity and inherent richness of the human mind and the collective human experience.

I genuinely hope you find as much enjoyment and revelation in reading this book as I did. May it inspire you to live a life that is not just fulfilling and satisfying, but truly aligned with the magnificent urgency and identity of your DDD neurotype.

# Preface

In this vibrant, relentless hum of a city, where every face is a fleeting brushstroke and time itself seems to accelerate, I often feel a profound, solitary echo. A deep knowing that I am not alone in this sensation, even when the loneliness presses in like the noise and the lights, a symphony played without a familiar score.

A dog barks at the moon, a sound sharp against the urban thrum. A man glances at his hand, a fleeting memory of a father's gentle touch, the world held safely in a small palm, the exhilarating view from the top. He was fearless then, adventurous. Now, this city feels like a foreign film without subtitles, its rhythm elusive, its conversations a boiling pot of incoherent snippets: "How are you? How much is it? What time is it? What's going on? Who believes them? See you later."

The stairs are slippery, steep, a treacherous climb where a single misstep can send you sliding down the ice. The screens flash warnings of dangers on the road, yet the deepest fear isn't of external peril. It's the chilling dread of losing the capacity to feel anything at all. To have the world's sensory richness fade: the fragrance of a hidden flower, the distinct smell of the city after rain, the lively hum of mopeds, the simple joy of pizza. To lose the profound emotional tapestry: a mother's unshed tears, a student's audacious dreams, the silent promise of encounters waiting in a bustling square.

To stand with antennas reaching for the sky, attuned to a frequency others seem to miss, yet find yourself alone at the crowd's edge. To become an outcast not by intention, but by a stumble, a genuine mistake in a world unforgiving of difference. A colossal sign promises, "It's all around you." But when you search, truly search, there is an emptiness.

This old world, it holds together only by the sheer, audacious courage of those who still dare to fall in love. To fall in love with life, with an idea, with a connection. That is the true music that pulses through our veins, a rhythm that compels us to wake, to rise, to push past complaint. This, then, is the only danger I genuinely fear: the loss of that heartbeat in my chest, the extinguishing of that fierce passion that fuels a project's growth, the dulling of hunger, thirst, the relentless evolution within. To lose the electric current of authentic contact, the raw impulse to laugh and to cry, to dissolve into the boundless sky and yet remain grounded in the earth's honest mud.

*This is my prelude to a journey of discovery.*

# Acknowledgments

I extend my heartfelt gratitude to the individuals and organizations whose invaluable contributions made this project a reality.

First and foremost, my sincere appreciation goes to the **Microsoft team**. Their unwavering guidance, insightful feedback, and steadfast support were instrumental throughout this endeavor. They generously shared their profound expertise, innovative insights, and essential resources, serving not just as colleagues, but as true mentors, collaborators, and friends.

I am also profoundly indebted to **Bill Gates**, a visionary leader, unparalleled philanthropist, and relentless innovator. Beyond his public impact, he has been a personal mentor, a source of endless inspiration, and a cherished role model. He instilled in me the profound value of curiosity, boundless creativity, and deep compassion, demonstrating the transformative power of technology to uplift humanity. His quiet encouragement in my academic and professional pursuits, and his unwavering belief in pursuing passions, have been a constant, perhaps even unknowing, beacon. I admire not only his monumental achievements but also the integrity and humility with which he wields such influence, always exemplifying generosity and an uncompromising commitment to integrity. This project would simply not have been possible without their collective help and encouragement. Their contribution and inspiration are deeply cherished.

My sincere thanks also go to the **Google team** for their exceptional help and seamless cooperation. Their generosity in sharing cutting-edge data, powerful tools, and extensive knowledge was invaluable. Their responsiveness and flexibility in navigating any challenges that arose demonstrated remarkable professionalism and a true spirit of partnership. They consistently exemplified collaboration and innovation, significantly advancing the frontiers of technology and contributing immensely to the successful realization of this work. Their pivotal partnership and steadfast support are profoundly appreciated.

# I

# Part One

# 1

# The Unseen Dimension: Living in Another Reality

Have you ever felt like an anomaly? Like the world operates on a frequency you can't quite tune into, or that you're living in a dimension just slightly askew from everyone else's? This persistent sense of being an outsider, a misfit in a world not quite designed for you, is a profound and often isolating experience.

Perhaps you perceive the world with an amplified sensitivity – emotions run deeper, sensations ignite more vividly, and thoughts cascade with remarkable speed. The joy and pain of others resonate with uncanny intensity, and the world's beauty and wonder strike you with a fresh, almost childlike awe.

This innate intensity often clashes with societal norms and unspoken rules, leaving you to navigate a world that feels inherently unsuited to your operating system. You might struggle to follow routines that others take for granted, or to truly connect with those who simply don't understand your unique perspective. The stress and chaos of everyday life can feel overwhelming, a constant pressure on your senses.

Yet, within this struggle lies a profound wellspring of creativity, intelligence, intuition, and a unique charm that you've honed not just to survive, but to truly thrive and leave your distinct mark. You've used your imagination to navigate the unknown, your humor to mask insecurities, and your talents to make a difference.

If any of this resonates, take a breath. You are not alone. You are not crazy, broken, or defective. You are, in fact, **neurodivergent**.

Neurodivergence describes the vast, natural variations in human brains, encompassing differences in sociability, learning, attention, mood, and other cognitive functions. It includes conditions like autism spectrum disorder (ASD), attention deficit hyperactivity disorder (ADHD), dyslexia, dyspraxia, Tourette syndrome, and many more. Simply put, neurodivergent individuals experience and interact with the world differently from those considered "neurotypical" – whose brain functions align with societal norms.

Crucially, being neurodivergent is not a disease, a defect, or something to be "cured." It doesn't diminish your worth or constrain your potential. Instead, it is a fundamental, natural variation of human diversity – a unique aspect that shapes your identity, enriches your experience, and imbues you with distinct perspectives and abilities. It is both a profound gift and a persistent challenge.

In "Bridging the Reality Gap," I invite you on my own deeply personal journey of discovering and ultimately embracing my neurodivergent self. Through shared insights and practical strategies learned along the way, my aim is to empower you to embark on a similar path. You'll also meet incredible neurodivergent individuals whose contributions across diverse fields stand as powerful testaments to the strength inherent in difference.

**This book is for you if:**

- You suspect or know that you are neurodivergent, or you want to learn more about neurodiversity.
- You want to understand yourself better and accept yourself more.
- You want to find your purpose and passion in life.
- You want to connect with others who share your experience and support your growth.
- You want to celebrate your neurodivergence and unleash your potential.

**This book is not for you if:**

- You believe that neurodivergence is a problem or a defect that needs to be eliminated or corrected.
- You want to conform to the neurotypical standards and expectations at the expense of your authenticity and happiness.
- You want to deny or hide your neurodivergence and pretend to be someone else.
- You want to isolate yourself from others who are different from you or who challenge you.
- You want to blame your neurodivergence for all your difficulties and failures.

## *Subchapter 1: The Unseen Current: Navigating the Early Storm*

From my earliest memories, I felt out of sync with my peers. Sitting still was an alien concept, attention a fleeting guest, and instructions often dissolved before reaching my full comprehension. I was the child easily distracted, impulsively speaking out, constantly moving, and perpetually forgetting homework – traits that invariably led to being "in trouble." The unspoken message was clear: I didn't fit the mold.

This dissonance extended to my own home. My parents, trying their best within their understanding, perceived me as lazy, rebellious, or disrespectful. Their constant nagging, scolding, and punishment for my "failures" only deepened my sense of alienation. They struggled to appreciate the wellspring of creativity, boundless curiosity, and genuine enthusiasm that defined me, focusing instead on my inability to conform to tasks like studying, cleaning, and organizing.

School proved to be another battlefield. Teachers, burdened by structured curricula, swiftly labeled me a "problem child," a "troublemaker," a "nuisance." My strengths went unnoticed, my weaknesses amplified. I endured endless, tedious assignments and tests, designed for a different kind of mind, leaving my unique learning style, interests, and burgeoning goals utterly unsupported.

I felt caught in a relentless storm of negativity, rejection, and profound frustration. Each day was a battle against a suffocating sea of expectations, rigid rules, and harsh judgments. It was as if I was trapped in an invisible cage, defined by limitations, failures, and pervasive disappointment.

Desperate, I wrestled with the unspoken question: What was fundamentally wrong with me? Why couldn't I simply "be like everyone else"? I lacked the tools to cope with the maelstrom of my emotions, challenges, and unspoken needs. At that time, I simply didn't know: I had ADHD.

## Subchapter 2: Finding My Frequency: Rebuilding and Redefining

The journey from that storm to clarity was far from easy, yet undeniably possible. Every misstep, every struggle, became a crucial lesson; every success, every moment of joy, a beacon. I learned, definitively, that ADHD is not a curse to bear, but a unique facet of my being—a wellspring of distinctive abilities, perspectives, and passions that profoundly shape who I am.

More profoundly, I recognized that ADHD is not an excuse for inaction, but an invitation to a unique set of challenges. It demands heightened self-awareness, deep mindfulness, unwavering self-compassion, and immense resilience. It necessitates a delicate balance of integrated strategies: medication, therapy, coaching, and intentional lifestyle adjustments. Above all, it calls for radical self-acceptance, self-love, and fierce self-advocacy.

And perhaps most liberating, I discovered that ADHD is not a solitary journey, but a shared odyssey. It has forged profound connections with others who share this neurotype or who genuinely seek to understand it. This shared space has become a platform to exchange stories, insights, and wisdom, allowing me to inspire, support, and learn from countless fellow travelers.

This book is my extended hand to you. It's my heartfelt assurance that you are not alone, not hopeless, not worthless. You are, in fact, incredibly amazing, powerfully capable, and immensely valuable. More than a memoir, a reflection, or a celebration, "Bridging the Reality Gap" is an invitation to join me on this intricate, exhilarating, and sometimes turbulent roller coaster ride of life with ADHD. It's an encouragement to buckle up, hold on tight, and truly *experience* the journey— embracing both the storms and the refuges, the soaring highs and the challenging lows, the obstacles and the boundless opportunities. This is not a rigid manual, a definitive scientific treatise, or a magic formula. It is, instead, a deeply personal story, an honest confession of vulnerability and triumph, and an optimistic vision for a future where neurodivergence is understood and celebrated. It is a work in progress, a work of art, and above all, a work of love.

While moments of stress or sadness are universal, when these feelings become overwhelming and disrupt your daily life, it's a clear signal to seek support. You are not meant to suffer in solitude. A wealth of resources and treatments exists for individuals with ADHD and related conditions, empowering you to manage symptoms, navigate challenges, and dramatically enhance your quality of life.

Within these pages, you will discover:

- How to decipher the often-hidden signs of ADHD that might be holding you back.
- A deeper understanding of the causes and far-reaching effects of your ADHD symptoms.
- Pathways to finding the right diagnosis and comprehen-

sive treatment tailored to your needs.
- Strategies to dismantle common myths and overcome the pervasive stigma surrounding ADHD.
- Practical approaches to cultivating healthy habits and sustainable routines that genuinely support your well-being.
- Tools to build more positive relationships and master effective communication skills.
- Methods for setting realistic, achievable goals and celebrating your progress, big and small.
- The profound art of celebrating your unique strengths and acknowledging your accomplishments.
- And ultimately, how to wholeheartedly embrace your neurodivergent uniqueness and unleash your boundless creativity.

This book is for you if you live with ADHD, or if you know and love someone who does. It's for you if you yearn to understand ADHD more profoundly, to appreciate its complexities and gifts. It's for you if you're ready to share in moments of laughter, tears, and profound personal growth. This book is for you if you're ready to join me on this remarkable journey, to truly "bridge the reality gap."

My deepest hope is that this book will illuminate the extraordinary beauty and inherent power of your neurodivergence, and inspire you to cultivate a fulfilling and deeply meaningful life.

Let's begin our journey together.

Are you ready?

2

# The Invisible Burden: Unmasking ADHD and the Weight of Stigma

*Section 1: Introduction: Decoding ADHD and its Unseen Challenges*

Attention Deficit Hyperactivity Disorder (ADHD) is far more than a simple inability to pay attention or an excess of restless energy. It is a common and complex neurodevelopmental condition, profoundly impacting millions worldwide across every stage of life. Characterized by persistent patterns of inattention, hyperactivity, and impulsivity, ADHD can profoundly interfere with daily functioning and development, touching every aspect from academic performance and professional productivity to personal relationships and holistic well-being.

Yet, the challenges faced by individuals with ADHD are not solely dictated by their symptoms. An equally significant, often more insidious, battle is waged against the pervasive stigma and discrimination that unjustly surround the disorder. This societal misunderstanding, often rooted in misinformation or a lack of empathy, frequently compounds the inherent difficulties of ADHD, creating additional, unnecessary layers of distress and hardship.

The American Psychiatric Association (APA) defines ADHD as "a persistent pattern of inattention and/or hyperactivity-impulsivity that interferes with functioning or development." While this clinical definition provides a framework, the lived experience of ADHD is far more nuanced and diverse. Symptoms manifest uniquely in each individual, typically including struggles with sustaining focus, organizing tasks, following multi-step instructions, recalling details, controlling impulses, and regulating intense emotions. The internal experience can range from a relentless, racing mind to a profound difficulty initiating tasks, from an overwhelming sensitivity to external stimuli to an internal restlessness that belies a calm exterior. These challenges usually emerge in childhood but can persist, and often intensify, into adolescence and adulthood, with many individuals receiving a diagnosis only much later in life due to factors such as limited awareness, unequal access to specialized services, or the masking effect of co-occurring conditions.

Globally, ADHD prevalence is estimated at approximately 5% in children and 2.5% in adults. However, these figures are dynamic, fluctuating based on diagnostic criteria, methodologies, and the specific populations studied, underscoring the variability in how the condition is identified and understood across different regions and cultures. The precise origins of ADHD remain multifaceted and are still being fully elucidated, though current understanding points to a complex interplay of genetic, environmental, and developmental factors. Identified risk factors include a family history of ADHD, prenatal exposure to substances like alcohol or tobacco, low birth weight, certain brain injuries, exposure to environmental toxins such as lead, and various forms of psychosocial adversity during crucial developmental periods. This complex etiology highlights that ADHD is a biologically rooted condition, not a mere behavioral choice or a consequence of poor parenting.

Diagnosing ADHD is a comprehensive and intricate process, demanding more than a single test. It involves a thorough clinical assessment, incorporating detailed interviews with the individual and often their family members, direct behavioral observations, the use of standardized rating scales completed by multiple informants (parents, teachers, partners), and psychological tests designed to evaluate cognitive functions like attention and executive skills. A definitive diagnosis requires that symptoms are present before the age of 12, occur consistently in more than one setting (e.g., home, school, work), cause significant impairment in major life domains, and cannot be better explained by another mental health condition. This rigorous process is crucial to differentiate ADHD from other conditions with overlapping symptoms, ensuring an accurate diagnosis and appropriate support.

The treatment of ADHD is almost universally multimodal, reflecting its complexity and the diverse ways it impacts an individual's life. This holistic approach typically integrates a combination of medication, psychotherapy, targeted be-havioral interventions, educational support, and intentional lifestyle adjustments.

- **Medication:** Often considered a cornerstone of treatment, medications for ADHD primarily include stimulants (such as methylphenidate or amphetamines) and non-stimulants. Stimulants work by increasing the availability of key neurotransmitters like dopamine and norepinephrine in the brain, which are vital for regulating attention, motivation, and reward pathways. For many, these medications can significantly reduce symptoms of inattention, hyperactivity, and impulsivity, providing a clearer mental landscape. However, individual responses vary, and potential side effects, such as appetite suppression, insomnia, headaches, irritability, anxiety, or cardiovascular considerations, necessitate careful monitoring and titration by a qualified healthcare professional. Non-stimulants offer an alternative for those who don't respond to or tolerate stimulants, working through different neurological mechanisms to improve symptom management.
- **Psychotherapy:** Beyond medication, psychotherapy plays a crucial role in helping individuals with ADHD develop coping mechanisms, improve emotional regulation, enhance self-esteem, refine social skills, and master organizational and time management strategies. Common therapeutic modalities include:
- **Cognitive-Behavioral Therapy (CBT):** Focuses on identifying and modifying unhelpful thought patterns and behaviors that contribute to ADHD-related challenges.
- **Dialectical Behavior Therapy (DBT):** Particularly helpful for emotional dysregulation, teaching skills in mindfulness, distress tolerance, emotion regulation, and interpersonal effectiveness.
- **Mindfulness-Based Therapy (MBT):** Cultivates present-

moment awareness and acceptance, helping individuals with ADHD to observe thoughts and feelings without being overwhelmed by them.

- **Family Therapy (FT):** Aims to improve communication and relationships within the family system, addressing how ADHD impacts family dynamics.
- **ADHD Coaching:** While not strictly therapy, coaching offers practical, goal-oriented support for executive function deficits, accountability, and strategy development.
- **Behavioral Interventions:** These involve applying principles of positive reinforcement (like praise or rewards) and negative consequences (such as time-out or loss of privileges) to shape desirable behaviors and reduce challenging ones. Effective at home and in educational settings, these interventions empower children with ADHD to follow rules, complete tasks, cooperate with peers, and improve impulse control. For adults, behavioral strategies often involve creating structured environments, using external cues, and developing consistent routines.
- **Educational Support and Workplace Accommodations:** Recognizing that traditional environments are often not designed for neurodivergent brains, educational and workplace accommodations are essential. These may include preferential seating, extended time for assignments or tests, reduced workload, frequent breaks, visual aids, auditory cues, and individualized instruction plans. In the workplace, this could translate to flexible hours, quiet workspaces, detailed written instructions, or the use of specific organizational tools. Such support ensures that individuals with ADHD can learn and work effectively, capitalizing on their strengths without being

unfairly disadvantaged by their challenges.

- **Lifestyle Changes:** Adopting healthy habits significantly contributes to managing ADHD symptoms and enhancing overall well-being. This includes engaging in regular physical exercise, maintaining a balanced and nutritious diet, ensuring adequate and consistent sleep patterns, implementing effective stress management techniques (like meditation or hobbies), and avoiding substances such as excessive alcohol or illicit drugs, which can exacerbate ADHD symptoms.

The outcomes for individuals with ADHD are highly variable, influenced by the severity of symptoms, the timeliness and effectiveness of intervention, and the presence of comorbid conditions. Learning disabilities, anxiety disorders, mood disorders, substance use disorders, and conduct disorders frequently co-occur with ADHD, complicating diagnosis and treatment and increasing the risk of negative life outcomes such as academic struggles, social isolation, unemployment, and even more serious issues like criminality or suicide. However, it is crucial to emphasize that ADHD does not equate to a predetermined poor outcome. With early, appropriate, and ongoing intervention, support, and guidance, many individuals with ADHD achieve remarkable success and satisfaction in their personal and professional lives, demonstrating immense resilience and tapping into their unique strengths.

One of the most profound factors influencing these outcomes is **stigma**. Stigma, in its essence, is a negative social attitude that devalues and marginalizes a group of people based on a perceived attribute or characteristic. For those with ADHD, stigma manifests as prejudice, stereotyping, social rejection, and outright discrimination. It can emanate from various sources: the general public, immediate family members, friends, educators, employers, healthcare professionals, and even, tragically, from within themselves (internalized stigma). The harmful effects of stigma are far-reaching, eroding self-esteem, undermining well-being, and diminishing overall quality of life. Furthermore, stigma acts as a significant barrier, discouraging individuals from seeking and receiving the crucial diagnosis, treatment, and support they need, perpetuating a vicious cycle of struggle and misunderstanding.

In this chapter, we will delve deeper into the intricate ways in which society perceives and evaluates ADHD. We will explore cutting-edge research shedding light on public understanding and the effectiveness of different approaches to fostering empathy. Crucially, we will provide practical tips and advice on how to navigate and cope with the pervasive impact of ADHD-related stigma. Finally, we will share compelling personal stories and experiences from individuals living with ADHD, highlighting their resilience, unique strengths, notable achievements, and their fervent call for greater societal understanding and acceptance. By the end of this chapter, our aim is to equip you with a deeper insight into both the challenges and the remarkable opportunities inherent in living with ADHD within a society still grappling with its full understanding.

## Section 2: Public Perception of ADHD: Bridging the Empathy Gap

How do individuals without ADHD truly perceive and understand the disorder? What are their reactions and assumptions when encountering someone with ADHD, and how do these perceptions ripple through the lives of those directly affected? These are not merely academic questions but deeply personal ones, which researchers have diligently pursued in their efforts to map the terrain of public perception regarding ADHD.

One powerful method employed in this research is **simulation**. Simulation involves immersing people without ADHD in an experience designed to mimic the internal and external realities of living with the condition. This can take various forms, from carefully crafted scenarios and evocative videos to immersive audio experiences or even sophisticated virtual reality (VR) environments. The core purpose of simulation is to cultivate empathy and provide a visceral insight into the daily struggles and unique challenges faced by individuals with ADHD. By putting themselves, even vicariously, in someone else's shoes, participants can move beyond abstract knowledge to a more profound, felt understanding.

However, it is crucial to acknowledge that simulation, while powerful, comes with inherent limitations. It can only ever offer a glimpse, not the full, multifaceted complexity and diversity of the ADHD experience, which varies widely from person to person. There's also a delicate balance to strike, as poorly designed simulations could inadvertently induce negative emotions or reinforce pre-existing biases towards ADHD, rather than fostering genuine understanding.

Furthermore, a simulated environment, by its very nature, may not fully capture the unpredictable, real-life contexts and nuanced social interactions that define the daily lives of people with ADHD.

In this section, we will explore the compelling results of a landmark study that harnessed the power of virtual reality to investigate how the general public simulates and evaluates the impairments associated with adult ADHD. This research, conducted by a collaborative team of researchers from Australia and Germany, aimed not only to measure perception but also to inform strategies for reducing stigma and improving public awareness.

The study recruited 60 participants from the general public, all of whom reported no prior diagnosis of ADHD or any other mental health disorder, ensuring a baseline of neurotypical perception. Participants were carefully randomized into one of three distinct groups: a control group, a simulation group, and an information group.

The **control group** served as a baseline; they received no specific intervention beyond completing an initial question-naire designed to gauge their existing knowledge, attitudes, and beliefs about ADHD.

The **simulation group** underwent an immersive virtual re-ality intervention. Donning a head-mounted display, these par-ticipants were transported into a vivid, 360-degree video de-piction of a typical day in the life of an adult living with ADHD. The experience was made profoundly personal through the narration of an individual with ADHD, who articulated their thoughts, feelings, and internal struggles as events unfolded. The video unfolded through a series of relatable scenes: the chaos of waking up late and rushing, the frustration of forgetting crucial appointments, the exasperation of misplacing essential items, the pressures of making mistakes at work, navigating difficult arguments with colleagues, and the pervasive sense of being overwhelmed and perpetually frustrated. This carefully constructed narrative, lasting approximately 15 minutes, aimed to create an embodied sense of the internal chaos and external challenges of ADHD.

In parallel, the **information group** received a more traditional educational intervention. They engaged with a detailed PowerPoint presentation that delivered factual, evidence-based information about adult ADHD, covering its definition, global prevalence, underlying causes, varied symptoms, diagnostic processes, multimodal treatments, and potential long-term outcomes. Crucially, the presentation also actively addressed common myths and pervasive misconceptions about ADHD, aiming to provide a clear and accurate understanding. This educational session also spanned approximately 15 minutes.

Following their respective interventions, all participants, across all three groups, completed a follow-up questionnaire that re-measured their knowledge, attitudes, and beliefs concerning ADHD. Additionally, they completed a separate questionnaire specifically designed to assess their levels of empathy for individuals living with ADHD.

The results of this study were illuminating. As expected, both the simulation group and the information group demonstrated a significant improvement in their factual knowledge about ADHD compared to the control group. This reinforced the idea that both experiential learning and traditional education can effectively convey information. However, the most compelling finding was that the **simulation group exhibited**

**significantly higher levels of empathy for people with ADHD** than both the information group and the control group. Furthermore, the simulation group also developed more positive attitudes towards individuals with ADHD compared to the other two groups.

These findings carry profound implications for our efforts to reduce stigma and improve public awareness of ADHD. They suggest that while factual information is important, direct, embodied experiences – even simulated ones – are far more potent in fostering genuine empathy and shifting negative attitudes. This highlights the power of narrative and experiential learning over mere data dissemination. By allowing individuals to, however briefly, "walk in the shoes" of someone with ADHD, we can create a deeper understanding that transcends intellectual comprehension and touches the realm of emotional connection, paving the way for a more accepting and inclusive society.

*Section 3: Coping with Stigma: Strategies for Resilience and Empowerment*

Stigma, as we've established, is a pervasive force – a negative social judgment that devalues and marginalizes individuals based on a particular attribute. For those with ADHD, this translates into a relentless barrage of prejudice, stereotyping, social rejection, and outright discrimination. It can originate from diverse sources: the broad societal public, immediate family members, circles of friends, educators, employers, healthcare providers, and perhaps most painfully, it can be internalized, turning into self-stigma. The corrosive effects of stigma are devastating, eroding self-esteem, undermining psychological well-being, diminishing life quality, and erecting formidable barriers to seeking and receiving essential diagnosis, treatment, and support.

So, how can individuals with ADHD navigate this landscape of judgment and protect their sense of self-worth? How can they effectively counter the negative perceptions and reactions of others, and most importantly, cultivate an inner resilience that allows them to thrive despite external pressures? This section offers a comprehensive set of practical tips and advice for coping with ADHD-related stigma, addressing its various sources through proactive, empowering strategies.

1. **Embrace Self-Acceptance:** This is the foundational step. Self-acceptance means fully embracing who you are—strengths and weaknesses, abilities and challenges, triumphs and setbacks. It's not about resignation or settling for less; rather, it's about acknowledging and celebrating your unique neurodivergent wiring and inherent potential. By reducing internalized stigma (the negative beliefs you may hold about yourself due to societal messages), you can significantly boost your self-confidence and self-esteem. Practice self-compassion by treating yourself with the same kindness and understanding you would offer a friend. Challenge negative self-talk and reframe ADHD traits as aspects of your unique operating system rather than inherent flaws.

2. **Prioritize Self-Care:** This is not a luxury, but a vital component of resilience. Self-care encompasses actively nurturing your physical and mental health through healthy

habits that enhance well-being and daily functioning. Specific strategies for ADHD include:

- **Regular Exercise:** Proven to improve mood, reduce anxiety, and enhance cognitive functions like attention.
- **Balanced Nutrition:** A diet rich in whole foods supports brain health and stable energy levels.
- **Adequate, Consistent Sleep:** Critical for executive functions, emotional regulation, and overall cognitive performance. Establishing a consistent sleep routine is paramount.
- **Stress Management:** Incorporate mindfulness, meditation, deep breathing exercises, or hobbies that help you unwind and de-stress.
- **Substance Avoidance:** Minimize or avoid alcohol, nicotine, and illicit drugs, which can exacerbate ADHD symptoms and interfere with treatment.
- **Structured Routines:** Even though ADHD brains resist routine, establishing flexible, predictable structures for daily tasks can provide a vital sense of control and reduce decision fatigue.

1. **Harness the Power of Education:** Knowledge is empowerment. Educating yourself about ADHD and its multifaceted impact on your life is paramount. Understand its causes, diverse symptoms, diagnostic nuances, various treatment options, and long-term trajectories. This deep understanding enables you to debunk common myths and misconceptions, transforming you from a passive recipient of judgment into an informed advocate. Education also empowers you to make well-informed de-

cisions about your treatment and goals, and to articulate your needs and preferences more effectively to others. Consider authoritative sources, scientific literature, and reputable ADHD organizations.

2. **Embrace Advocacy:** Advocacy is about finding your voice and speaking up – for yourself and for others who share your condition. Personal advocacy involves asserting your rights and expressing your needs as an individual with ADHD in various contexts, whether with healthcare providers, in academic settings, or at work. It might mean requesting reasonable accommodations or explaining your working style. Broader advocacy involves raising awareness and fostering understanding of ADHD among the general public, family, friends, teachers, employers, healthcare professionals, and even policymakers. By challenging stigma and discrimination directly, you contribute to promoting positive change and fostering social justice for the entire ADHD community.

3. **Seek Support Groups:** Connecting with others who understand your experience is profoundly validating and empowering. Support groups offer a safe space where individuals with similar experiences or interests meet regularly to share information, practical advice, emotional support, and mutual encouragement. These groups can combat the isolation and loneliness that often accompany ADHD, providing empathy, validation, and a sense of belonging. Learning from others who have successfully navigated similar challenges can offer invaluable strategies and renewed hope.

4. **Engage in Therapy:** Therapy provides a structured, guided process with a trained professional to address the

emotional, psychological, and behavioral aspects of living with ADHD and its associated stigma. Therapy can help process the negative emotions stemming from stigma, such as anger, sadness, shame, guilt, fear, and anxiety. It can also improve self-esteem, enhance well-being, and develop crucial coping skills, problem-solving abilities, and realistic goal-setting strategies. Cognitive-behavioral therapy (CBT), dialectical behavior therapy (DBT), and ADHD-specific coaching are particularly effective in building the resilience needed to thrive despite stigma.

By actively integrating these strategies into your life, you can significantly reduce the insidious impact of stigma, enhancing your well-being, improving your functioning, and ultimately, bridging the reality gap between how you are perceived and who you truly are.

*Section 4: Stories of Americans with ADHD: Voices from the Front Lines of Stigma*

In this section, we move from clinical descriptions and coping strategies to the deeply personal. We will share compelling stories and lived experiences of Americans with ADHD who have bravely navigated the currents of stigma and discrimination. These narratives illuminate not only the profound challenges but also the remarkable resilience, unique strengths, notable achievements, and enduring hopes for a more understanding future.

Our first story introduces **John, a 35-year-old software**

**engineer thriving in the bustling heart of New York City.** John's journey began with a diagnosis of ADHD at age 10, following years of struggling to find his footing in school.

"I always felt like an alien in the classroom," John recalls, his voice tinged with a familiar weariness. "Paying attention was like trying to catch smoke. Staying on task felt impossible; my mind would dart to a thousand different things simultaneously. Following directions was a constant struggle, and completing assignments felt like scaling Everest without ropes. Every little sound, every flicker of light, was a distraction. I was also incredibly hyperactive and impulsive. Answers would blurt out before I'd even fully processed the question. I'd interrupt others mid-sentence, fidget incessantly, and found it physically painful to remain seated. The result? Constant scoldings, endless punishments, and frequent trips to the principal's office. I truly believed I was just a 'bad kid' who couldn't do anything right."

His parents, grappling with their own understanding, eventually took him to a psychologist, leading to his ADHD diagnosis and a prescription for medication. "The medication did help me calm down and focus, a little," John admits, "but it also left me feeling dull, muted, almost numb. I hated taking it, but there was no real choice. My parents and teachers insisted, saying it was 'for my own good,' a bitter pill to swallow for a spirited ten-year-old."

The external stigma was relentless. "Some classmates would tease me mercilessly, call me names like 'space cadet' or 'weirdo,' and explicitly exclude me from games and activities. Teachers, frustrated by my non-conformity, often doubted my diagnosis entirely, blaming my struggles on laziness, lack of motivation, or outright disrespect. Even some relatives weighed in, questioning my parents' decision to medicate me, whispering about 'overdiagnosis' or implying I was 'spoiled.' I carried a profound sense of shame and loneliness. All I wished for was to be 'normal' and for my ADHD to simply vanish."

Despite this arduous start, John's innate intelligence, boundless creativity, and tenacious work ethic enabled him to graduate from both high school and college with commendable grades. It was in the world of computer science and programming that he truly found his calling, discovering an environment uniquely suited to his ADHD traits of intense curiosity, innovative thinking, and innate problem-solving abilities.

"I was captivated by computers and technology from a young age," John explains, his passion evident. "They presented an endless frontier of fascination and challenge. They also became my refuge, a space where I could escape the noise of the 'real world' and construct my own. I taught myself to code at twelve, spending countless hours immersed in learning new languages, tools, and techniques. The online programming forums and global competitions became my social sphere, where my neurodivergent mind, with its capacity for deep hyperfocus, was a distinct advantage, not a hindrance."

His passion naturally led him to pursue a career in software engineering, a field where his unique cognitive profile proved invaluable. "I love my job," he states unequivocally. "It's challenging, deeply rewarding, and genuinely fun. It allows me to leverage my core strengths – creativity, innovation, and an almost obsessive drive to solve complex problems. Crucially, I have a high degree of autonomy, flexibility, and a constant influx of varied, stimulating projects. This environment provides the novelty and challenge my brain craves, preventing the mental stagnation that can be so debilitating."

Yet, even in a field seemingly tailor-made for his strengths, John acknowledges the ongoing, often subtle, challenges related to his ADHD in both his personal and professional life.

"I still grapple with executive functions," he admits. "Time management is often a fluid concept, deadlines can sneak up on me, and things frequently get misplaced. I often find myself starting numerous projects simultaneously, only to cycle through them rather than completing one linearly. Socially, there are still hurdles with communication, active listening, and consistently reading social cues. I might inadvertently say the wrong thing, miss subtle signals, or unintentionally offend someone. The world still sometimes feels 'off-kilter,' and there are moments I still wish for a neurotypical operating system."

The sting of stigma, though less overt than in his youth, also persists. "Some colleagues occasionally doubt my abilities or misinterpret my work style, attributing my non-linear approach to unreliability, unprofessionalism, or irresponsibility. Friends or family members, even with good intentions, sometimes struggle to fully grasp the nuances of my ADHD, leading them to view me as immature, selfish, or careless. Despite all my progress, there's still that lingering feeling of being 'different,' that occasional yearning for a 'normal' existence."

To navigate these ongoing challenges and the persistent echoes of stigma, John has meticulously developed and refined a suite of coping strategies over the years:

"To manage my ADHD symptoms and optimize my functioning, I rely heavily on external tools and specific techniques. For instance:

- **Time Management:** I meticulously use multiple calendars, set pervasive reminders, and employ alarms for every task, leveraging apps to keep track of deadlines and complex projects. My phone is constantly buzzing with prompts.
- **Organization:** Lists are my lifeblood, along with detailed notes, clearly labeled folders, and visual systems to organize my digital and physical workspaces, ensuring my belongings have a designated home (even if they occasionally wander).
- **Planning & Prioritization:** For larger projects, I break them down using charts, diagrams, mind maps, and even quick sketches to visualize the steps, sub-goals, and interdependencies.
- **Motivation & Focus:** I utilize timers (like the Pomodoro technique for focused bursts), build in immediate, small rewards for completing tasks, and curate specific playlists of music designed to enhance concentration. Regular short breaks are non-negotiable.
- **Distraction Control:** Noise-canceling headphones are my constant companion. I also use earplugs, adjust lighting with curtains, and employ 'do not disturb' signs (both digital and physical) to create a distraction-free bubble when deep work is required.

In confronting stigma, I leverage different but equally vital skills and resources to protect and enhance my self-image:

- **Education and Dissemination:** I make it my mission to learn everything I can about ADHD – its neurological basis, symptoms, diagnosis, and treatment. I then proactively share factual information with others who may hold misconceptions or simply lack understanding. I believe knowledge is the most powerful antidote to ignorance.

- **Self-Advocacy & Collective Advocacy:** I confidently articulate my needs and preferences as a person with ADHD in any given situation. Furthermore, I actively participate in raising awareness, understanding, and acceptance for the entire ADHD community among the general public, within educational institutions, in workplaces, and across healthcare systems."

*Section 5: Conclusion: Embracing the Neurodivergent Future*

In this comprehensive chapter, we have embarked on a journey to demystify Attention Deficit Hyperactivity Disorder, moving beyond its superficial symptoms to reveal its profound neurodevelopmental roots and pervasive impact. We have traversed the intricate landscape of ADHD, from its core definition, global prevalence, complex etiology, and diagnostic challenges, to the multifaceted approaches to treatment that offer hope and stability. Crucially, we have illuminated the often-overlooked yet devastating influence of stigma, underscoring its ability to devalue, marginalize, and create significant barriers for individuals living with ADHD.

Our exploration delved into the fascinating realm of public perception, highlighting a groundbreaking study that demonstrated the superior power of immersive virtual reality simulation over mere factual information in fostering genuine empathy and cultivating positive attitudes towards ADHD. This research offers a compelling roadmap for future awareness campaigns, emphasizing the transformative potential of experiential learning in bridging the societal empathy gap. Furthermore, we provided a vital toolkit of practical strategies for coping with stigma, empowering individuals to cultivate self-acceptance, prioritize self-care, engage in active education and advocacy, build supportive communities, and leverage therapeutic interventions.

Finally, through the poignant and resilient personal story of John, we have seen the lived reality of ADHD and stigma unfold – from childhood misunderstanding and the alienating pressure to conform, to the discovery of passion, the navigation of ongoing challenges, and the development of powerful coping mechanisms. John's narrative, like countless others, stands as a testament to the fact that ADHD, while presenting significant hurdles, is also intrinsically linked to unique strengths, profound creativity, and an incredible capacity for resilience.

Our hope is that this chapter has not only deepened your knowledge and understanding of ADHD and the pervasive nature of stigma but has also ignited within you a profound sense of empathy and a desire to actively support individuals with ADHD in both your personal and professional spheres. We encourage you to challenge outdated perceptions and actively dismantle the discrimination that people with ADHD too frequently encounter in various settings and situations.

The journey of "Bridging the Reality Gap" is one of mutual understanding, acceptance, and empowerment. Let us collectively strive to create a world where neurodivergence is not just tolerated, but truly celebrated as an integral and valuable aspect of human diversity.

If you are interested in learning more about ADHD and stigma, here are some suggestions for further reading and resources:

- **ADHD Awareness Month:** A comprehensive website providing information, resources, and events dedicated to ADHD awareness and advocacy.
- **ADHD Stigma: The Power of Words:** A powerful video that elucidates how our language choices profoundly impact the way we perceive and treat individuals with ADHD.
- **ADHD Voices:** A rich website featuring diverse stories and videos from individuals living with ADHD, offering varied backgrounds and perspectives.
- **Attention Deficit Disorder Association (ADDA):** A vital online resource offering robust support, extensive educational materials, and dedicated advocacy for adults with ADHD.
- **Children and Adults with Attention-Deficit/Hyperactivity Disorder (CHADD):** A leading national organization providing comprehensive information, valuable resources, and essential services for individuals with ADHD and their families.
- **How to Be an Ally to Someone with ADHD:** An insightful article offering practical tips and advice on how to be a supportive friend, partner, or colleague to someone living with ADHD.
- **Stigma Experienced by Adults with Attention-Deficit/Hyperactivity Disorder: A Systematic Review:** A

rigorous scientific paper that comprehensively reviews existing literature on the sources, types, effects, and effective coping strategies for stigma experienced by adults with ADHD.

# 3

# The Entrepreneurial Superpower: Harnessing ADHD for Innovation and Impact

You possess an extraordinary gift. It's a gift often misunderstood, frequently underestimated, and tragically, sometimes even maligned. Yet, when truly recognized and harnessed, it holds the potential to propel you into the realm of successful entrepreneurship, transforming what many perceive as a disadvantage into your most potent secret weapon. This gift is your Attention Deficit Hyperactivity Disorder – your ADHD.

ADHD is a complex neurodevelopmental condition, profoundly influencing how your brain processes information, regulates emotions, and manages impulses. It can indeed present significant challenges, making tasks that demand sustained focus, meticulous organization, long-term planning, and consistent follow-through feel like monumental uphill battles. The inherent wiring can also predispose you to a restless pursuit of novelty, making you susceptible to boredom, deep frustration, heightened anxiety, and episodes of depression when stimulation is lacking or when faced with tasks that don't align with your intrinsic motivation.

However, to view ADHD solely as a "disorder" is to miss its most profound truth. It is not merely a deficit; it is a fundamental difference in neurocognitive functioning. A difference that bestows upon you a unique constellation of strengths, abilities, and perspectives. It is precisely this distinct wiring that can empower you to conceive, launch, and passionately grow a business that resonates with your deepest convictions and ignites your boundless energy.

In this chapter, we embark on a transformative journey. We will delve into the very core of your ADHD, not to pathologize it, but to reclaim its narrative and illuminate how its inherent characteristics can be strategically leveraged, turning perceived weaknesses into undeniable advantages within the dynamic world of entrepreneurship. You will discover how to:

- **Unleash your boundless creativity** to generate groundbreaking ideas and devise ingenious solutions where others see only obstacles.
- **Fuel your insatiable curiosity** to relentlessly explore uncharted opportunities, identify nascent markets, and uncover overlooked niches.
- **Master the power of hyperfocus**, allowing you to immerse yourself with unparalleled intensity in your passion, bringing your grandest visions to vivid reality.

- **Forge an unyielding resilience** that transforms challenges and inevitable setbacks into powerful stepping stones for growth, propelling you forward through adversity.
- **Cultivate a calculated risk-taking mindset** that empowers you to seize fleeting chances, make decisive moves, and innovate beyond conventional boundaries.

Beyond celebrating these inherent strengths, this chapter will also equip you with the foresight and practical strategies necessary to navigate the potential pitfalls that might otherwise derail your entrepreneurial journey. You will learn how to:

- **Develop robust strategies** to effectively manage distractions and overcome the insidious grip of procrastination.
- **Establish empowering routines and streamlined systems** that bring order to your time, tasks, and creative chaos, fostering consistent productivity.
- **Actively seek vital support and constructive feedback** from a curated network of mentors, strategic partners, and understanding peers who resonate with your journey.
- **Achieve a sustainable equilibrium** between your professional ambitions and personal well-being, recognizing the critical role of self-care in long-term success.
- **Embrace and learn from failures**, transforming them from sources of despair into invaluable data points for continuous adaptation and exponential growth.

This book, and indeed this chapter, is far more than a conventional manual or a rigid business guide. It is a compelling narrative. It is a collection of inspiring stories from individuals like you, individuals with ADHD, who have not only achieved remarkable entrepreneurial success but have done so precisely *because* of their ADHD, utilizing it as a hidden, powerful advantage to realize their most ambitious dreams.

You will meet titans of industry and visionary founders who have undeniably shaped our modern world, all while navigating the unique landscape of ADHD. These are not merely abstract figures; they are living proof that your neurodivergent brain is not a barrier but a blueprint for breakthrough.

*Section 2: The ADHD Entrepreneurial Toolkit: Strengths Redefined*

The traditional view of ADHD often focuses on deficits: attention *deficit*, hyperactivity *disorder*. But within the entrepreneurial ecosystem, many of these "deficits" transform into potent advantages. The very traits that can cause challenges in conventional settings become superpowers in the right context. Let's redefine these characteristics and understand how they form your unique entrepreneurial toolkit.

1. Unleashed Creativity and Innovative Thinking:
2. The ADHD mind is a relentless idea generator. Unlike neurotypical brains that tend to follow more linear thought paths, the ADHD brain excels in divergent thinking – the ability to produce a wide range of unique and novel solutions to a problem. This means you are less constrained by conventional boundaries, more prone to "thinking outside the box," and highly adept at connecting

seemingly unrelated concepts.

- **How it Fuels Entrepreneurship:** Entrepreneurship demands fresh perspectives. Your brain's rapid-fire ideation and unconventional problem-solving make you a natural innovator. You're more likely to spot unmet needs, envision disruptive products or services, and devise creative marketing strategies. When faced with a roadblock, your mind instinctively seeks alternative routes, often leading to truly breakthrough solutions that a more rigid thinker might miss. This intrinsic ability to challenge the status quo and envision new possibilities is an unparalleled asset in a competitive market.

1. Boundless Curiosity and Relentless Exploration:
2. The constant quest for novelty, a hallmark of the ADHD brain, translates into an insatiable curiosity. You are driven to explore new ideas, delve into complex topics, and learn about diverse industries. This isn't just a casual interest; it's a deep-seated drive that pushes you to uncover every facet of a subject that captures your attention.

- **How it Fuels Entrepreneurship:** This relentless curiosity is invaluable for identifying new opportunities and understanding markets. You're the one who will research niche trends long before they go mainstream, intuitively grasp emerging technologies, or uncover overlooked customer segments. This investigative drive fuels effective market research, competitive analysis, and strategic positioning, allowing you to pivot quickly and adapt to evolving landscapes. Your inherent desire to understand "how things work" and "what else is possible" is a powerful engine for business growth and diversification.

1. The Power of Hyperfocus – The Flow State:
2. While often struggling with consistent attention on mundane tasks, when an ADHD individual is genuinely engaged and passionate about a subject, they can enter a state of hyperfocus. This intense, almost impenetrable concentration allows for hours of uninterrupted, highly productive work, often leading to mastery in specific areas. During hyperfocus, the external world fades, and the individual becomes completely absorbed in the task at hand.

- **How it Fuels Entrepreneurship:** Entrepreneurship is built on passion and sustained effort. When you find your entrepreneurial "spark," your hyperfocus becomes an incredible asset. You can dive deep into product development, master a new skill rapidly, or push through complex business challenges with unparalleled intensity. This capacity for deep work enables rapid prototyping, accelerated learning, and the ability to execute on a vision with single-minded devotion, outperforming those who might struggle to maintain such an intense level of engagement.

1. Unyielding Resilience and Rapid Adaptability:
2. Individuals with ADHD often spend a lifetime navigating a world that isn't built for their operating system. This constant need to adapt, troubleshoot, and bounce back

from setbacks (whether academic, social, or professional) cultivates an extraordinary level of resilience. You've learned to pick yourself up, pivot, and find alternative routes when conventional ones fail.

- **How it Fuels Entrepreneurship:** The entrepreneurial journey is fraught with challenges, unexpected obstacles, and inevitable failures. Your ingrained resilience means you're less likely to be deterred by setbacks. You possess a unique tenacity, an ability to tolerate uncertainty, and a remarkable capacity to adapt quickly to changing market conditions or unforeseen problems. Instead of crumbling under pressure, your brain is often wired to find innovative workarounds and adjust strategies on the fly, making you incredibly agile in dynamic business environments.

1. Calculated Risk-Taking and Bold Decisiveness:
2. The impulsivity often associated with ADHD, when channeled effectively, can translate into a beneficial willingness to take calculated risks and make bold decisions. You may be less prone to overthinking or analysis paralysis, and more willing to venture into uncharted territory, propelled by intuition and a desire for immediate action.

- **How it Fuels Entrepreneurship:** Startups and new ventures inherently involve risk. Your comfort with uncertainty and your readiness to act swiftly can give you a significant advantage. While not advocating for reckless behavior, the ability to step outside the comfort zone, seize fleeting opportunities, and make quick decisions can differentiate a successful entrepreneur from one who remains perpetually on the sidelines. This trait, tempered with experience and strategic foresight, becomes a potent force for pioneering new markets and disrupting established industries.

1. High Energy and Urgency:
2. Many with ADHD possess a seemingly boundless reserve of energy and an inherent sense of urgency, especially when engaged in tasks that excite them. This isn't just physical energy but a mental drive that propels them forward.

- **How it Fuels Entrepreneurship:** Launching and scaling a business demands immense energy, stamina, and a proactive approach. Your high energy can fuel long hours, intense work periods, and the sustained effort required to get a venture off the ground. The sense of urgency, when managed, can drive efficient execution and a constant push for progress, ensuring that opportunities are seized rather than missed.

By recognizing and strategically nurturing these inherent strengths, you begin to see your ADHD not as a "deficit" to be overcome, but as a "difference" to be leveraged—a powerful entrepreneurial toolkit waiting to be fully deployed.

## *Section 3: Navigating the Entrepreneurial Minefield: Managing ADHD Pitfalls*

While ADHD offers a formidable suite of entrepreneurial strengths, it's equally important to acknowledge and strategically manage its inherent challenges. These are not character flaws, but rather neurocognitive patterns that, left unaddressed, can indeed become "minefields" on your entrepreneurial path. The key is to transform awareness into actionable strategies, allowing you to mitigate potential pitfalls and sustain your momentum.

1. Conquering Distractions and Procrastination:
2. Executive dysfunction, particularly difficulty with task initiation and maintaining focus on unstimulating tasks, often manifests as chronic procrastination and susceptibility to distractions. The urgency of a looming deadline can trigger hyperfocus, but getting started is often the hardest part.

- **Strategic Solutions:**
- **Environmental Control:** Design your workspace for minimal distractions – noise-canceling headphones, a clear desk, turning off non-essential notifications, utilizing website blockers.
- **Body Doubling:** Work alongside a trusted friend, colleague, or accountability partner (even virtually). Their presence can provide subtle external regulation and motivation.
- **Gamification:** Turn tasks into a game. Set mini-

challenges, reward yourself for small completions, or use apps that incorporate game-like elements to sustain engagement.

- **Task Chunking:** Break down large, overwhelming tasks into the smallest possible, actionable steps. Focus only on the immediate next micro-step to overcome initiation paralysis.
- **The "Two-Minute Rule":** If a task takes less than two minutes, do it immediately. This prevents small tasks from piling up and becoming overwhelming mental clutter.
- **Urgency Creation:** For tasks you're not excited about, create artificial deadlines or commit to public declarations to generate the necessary pressure.

1. Establishing Order: Organization, Planning, and Follow-Through:
2. Challenges with working memory, organization, and the planning aspects of executive function can make maintaining consistent systems difficult. Entrepreneurship demands meticulous planning and reliable follow-through.

- **Strategic Solutions:**
- **Externalize Your Brain:** Rely heavily on external systems – calendars, digital planners, reminder apps, task management software (like Trello, Asana, Monday.com). Do not trust your memory for anything critical.
- **Simplify Systems:** Complex organizational systems will fail. Opt for minimalist, intuitive systems. One designated place for keys, wallet, phone. Digital notes over physical paper.

- **Visual Planning:** For project planning, use mind maps, flowcharts, or large whiteboards. Visual cues are often more effective for the ADHD brain than linear lists.
- **Scheduled "Planning Time":** Dedicate specific, short blocks each day or week solely for planning and organizing, rather than trying to do it on the fly.
- **Automate Where Possible:** Use automation tools for recurring tasks (e.g., billing, social media posting) to reduce mental load and ensure consistency.

1. The Power of Connection: Seeking Support and Feedback:
2. The entrepreneurial journey can be isolating, and the tendency to "go it alone" or fear judgment can prevent seeking crucial support.

- **Strategic Solutions:**
- **Build a Diverse Network:** Actively seek out mentors who understand business, ADHD, or both. Form alliances with co-founders or strategic partners whose strengths complement your weaknesses.
- **Join Peer Groups/Masterminds:** Engage with other entrepreneurs, especially those with ADHD, in formal or informal groups. Share challenges, gain insights, and provide mutual accountability.
- **Hire Support:** Don't hesitate to delegate tasks that drain your energy or exploit your weaknesses. Virtual assistants, bookkeepers, or administrative support can be invaluable.
- **Embrace Constructive Feedback:** Develop a mindset that views feedback as data for improvement, not personal criticism. Actively solicit it from trusted sources.

1. Sustained Energy: Work-Life Balance and Well-being:
2. The allure of hyperfocus combined with the intense demands of entrepreneurship can lead to burnout, neglecting self-care, and an imbalance that ultimately cripples productivity and mental health.

- **Strategic Solutions:**
- **Scheduled Breaks:** Intentionally schedule breaks throughout your workday – short "brain breaks," walks, or even quick bursts of physical activity.
- **Non-Negotiable Self-Care:** Treat self-care (exercise, nutritious meals, sufficient sleep, hobbies) as business-critical appointments in your calendar.
- **Set Boundaries:** Learn to say no to non-essential commitments. Define clear working hours and stick to them as much as possible.
- **Mindfulness and Stress Reduction:** Integrate short mindfulness practices into your day to help regulate emotions and reduce the impact of entrepreneurial stress.
- **Connect with Nature:** Spending time outdoors can significantly reduce mental fatigue and improve focus for individuals with ADHD.

1. Learning from the Labyrinth: Embracing Failures:
2. Given the trial-and-error nature of entrepreneurship and the ADHD brain's tendency to move quickly, failures are inevitable. The key is how you respond to them.

- **Strategic Solutions:**
- **Reframe Failure:** View setbacks as essential learning opportunities and data points for iteration, rather than

personal shortcomings. Every "failure" brings you closer to a solution.

- **Post-Mortem Analysis (Brief):** After a setback, conduct a quick, objective review: What happened? What was learned? What will be done differently next time? Avoid dwelling or self-criticism.
- **Celebrate Small Wins:** The ADHD brain thrives on novelty and immediate gratification. Celebrate every small achievement to maintain motivation and momentum, building resilience.
- **Seek Perspective:** Talk through challenges with your support network. An external perspective can help you see solutions or reframe situations more constructively.

By proactively addressing these common ADHD pitfalls with tailored strategies, you can transform potential stumbling blocks into guardrails, allowing your entrepreneurial strengths to shine and propel you towards sustainable success.

## *Section 4: Trailblazers: Inspiring ADHD Entrepreneurs*

The idea that ADHD can be an entrepreneurial superpower is not merely theoretical; it's vividly demonstrated by a lineage of extraordinary individuals who have leveraged their unique neurocognitive profiles to build empires, revolutionize industries, and leave an indelible mark on the world. These trailblazers are not exceptions to the rule; they are compelling proof of what's possible when ADHD is recognized, understood, and strategically channeled.

Let's look at some of these inspiring figures:

Richard Branson: The Visionary Rebel of Virgin Group

Richard Branson, the iconic founder of Virgin Group, is arguably one of the most recognizable and outspoken entrepreneurs with dyslexia and ADHD. His journey is a testament to how a rejection of conventional education can fuel revolutionary business models. Branson dropped out of school at 16, unable to conform to the rigid academic structure that failed to engage his neurodivergent mind. His dyslexia, which caused him significant struggles in reading and writing, pushed him to develop powerful oral communication skills and an exceptional ability to delegate tasks, surrounding himself with people who excelled where he struggled.

- **ADHD Advantage:** Branson's ADHD fuels his **boundless curiosity and unyielding drive for novelty**, leading him to launch over 400 companies across wildly diverse industries – from music and airlines to telecommunications and space tourism. His **impulsivity**, often seen as a drawback, translates into **bold, decisive moves** that disrupt markets and seize opportunities before competitors can react. His **disdain for bureaucracy and conventional rules** makes him a natural disruptor, constantly challenging the status quo. His high energy allows him to juggle multiple ventures simultaneously, while his **charismatic personality and authenticity** enable him to build strong personal brands and cultivate fierce loyalty.

David Neeleman: Revolutionizing Air Travel with Relentless Innovation

David Neeleman, the visionary founder of JetBlue Airways

and multiple other airlines, is another prominent figure who openly attributes much of his success to his ADHD. His neurodivergent brain is constantly seeking improvement and efficiency, leading to customer-centric innovations that transformed the airline industry.

- **ADHD Advantage:** Neeleman's **hyperfocus** on customer experience and operational efficiency drove him to meticulously rethink every aspect of air travel, from seat design to booking processes. His **restlessness and constant pursuit of novelty** mean he's never satisfied with the status quo; he's perpetually looking for ways to make things better, faster, and more customer-friendly. His **divergent thinking** allowed him to see solutions where others saw only problems, such as offering live TV on flights or simplifying fare structures. His high energy and drive enabled him to launch multiple successful airlines, demonstrating an unparalleled capacity for sustained entrepreneurial effort.

Barbara Corcoran: From Single Loan to Real Estate Empire
Barbara Corcoran, best known for her role on Shark Tank, built The Corcoran Group into a billion-dollar real estate business from a mere $1,000 loan. While not formally diagnosed with ADHD until later in life, she openly discusses how her traits align with the condition, particularly her boundless energy and unique approach to business.

- **ADHD Advantage:** Corcoran's **high energy and infectious enthusiasm** are key to her sales prowess and ability to motivate teams. Her **impulsivity**, when channeled, translates into quick, decisive actions in a fast-paced market. Her **ability to connect authentically with people** and build rapport quickly is crucial in relationship-driven industries like real estate. She thrives on novelty and excitement, which kept her constantly innovating her sales strategies and expanding her business. Her resilience, honed by early struggles, allowed her to overcome numerous setbacks and build her empire brick by brick.

Ingvar Kamprad: The Visionary Behind IKEA's Global Simplicity

Ingvar Kamprad, the Swedish founder of IKEA, created the world's largest furniture retailer based on a philosophy of simple, affordable design and self-assembly. Though ADHD was not a recognized diagnosis in his youth, his well-documented traits align with many aspects of the condition, including his unconventional thinking and deep dives into specific interests.

- **ADHD Advantage:** Kamprad's **unconventional approach to business** and disdain for complex, high-cost models led to the revolutionary flat-pack furniture concept. His **intense focus on efficiency and frugality**, characteristic of a certain type of ADHD hyperfocus, allowed him to optimize every aspect of the supply chain to drive down costs. His **innovative thinking** saw an opportunity to empower customers to assemble their own furniture, a concept that was radical at the time but became a global phenomenon. His single-minded dedication to his vision, despite early skepticism, is a hallmark of channeling neurodivergent drive.

John T. Chambers: Leading Cisco Through the Internet Revolution

John T. Chambers, the former CEO of Cisco Systems, famously led the company through the explosive growth of the internet era, transforming it into a networking technology giant. Chambers has spoken publicly about his dyslexia and ADHD, and how these conditions shaped his leadership style.

- **ADHD Advantage:** Chambers's **rapid information processing and ability to connect disparate ideas** allowed him to quickly grasp emerging technologies and market trends. His **high energy and relentless drive** enabled him to maintain an incredibly demanding schedule and lead a rapidly expanding global company. His experience with dyslexia reportedly sharpened his listening skills and ability to grasp the "big picture" rather than getting bogged down in minutiae. This holistic, visionary approach, combined with his **fearless embrace of change and innovation**, was crucial in guiding Cisco through multiple technological shifts.

These individuals are not mere anomalies. They are powerful role models, demonstrating that ADHD, far from being a limitation, can be a profound catalyst for entrepreneurial success. Their stories are a testament to the fact that when you understand, embrace, and strategically harness your unique neurodivergent operating system, you can achieve your grandest ambitions. You possess what it takes to be an entrepreneur. You have ADHD. And that, unequivocally, is your advantage.

## *Section 5: Conclusion: Your Entrepreneurial Blueprint*

In this chapter, we have fundamentally shifted the narrative surrounding ADHD in the context of entrepreneurship. We have moved beyond a deficit-focused view to illuminate the profound and often overlooked advantages that neurodivergent minds bring to the world of business. We've explored how traits like boundless creativity, insatiable curiosity, laser-like hyperfocus, unyielding resilience, and a propensity for calculated risk-taking are not merely characteristics of ADHD, but powerful entrepreneurial superpowers.

We also navigated the potential challenges that these very strengths can sometimes present, offering a comprehensive toolkit of strategic solutions for managing distractions, cultivating organization, building robust support networks, nurturing essential work-life balance, and transforming setbacks into invaluable learning experiences. The journey highlighted by trailblazing entrepreneurs like Richard Branson, David Neeleman, Barbara Corcoran, Ingvar Kamprad, and John T. Chambers serves as a compelling testament to the immense potential unlocked when ADHD is viewed as a blueprint for innovation, rather than a barrier to success. Their stories underscore that the very "differences" of ADHD can be the secret sauce for disrupting industries, creating unique value, and achieving extraordinary impact.

Your neurodivergent brain is not a hurdle; it is your unique entrepreneurial blueprint. It equips you with the raw material for innovation, the drive for relentless pursuit, and the adaptability to thrive in dynamic environments. The path of entrepreneurship is inherently suited to a mind that thrives on novelty, problem-solving, and building something from the ground up.

As we conclude this chapter, remember that this book, "Bridging the Reality Gap," is designed to be your companion on this remarkable journey. It is structured to provide you with the foundational understanding, the practical strategies, and the inspiring validation you need to unleash your full potential.

The remainder of this book is organized as follows:

- **Chapter 1: What is ADHD?** This chapter provides an overview of the definition, prevalence, causes, symptoms, diagnosis, treatment, and outcomes of ADHD. It also explains how ADHD affects different aspects of life, such as work, school, relationships, and health.
- **Chapter 2: What is stigma?** This chapter introduces the concept of stigma and its impact on people with ADHD. It also describes the sources, types, effects, and coping strategies of stigma experienced by people with ADHD.
- **Chapter 3: How can ADHD be an advantage?** This chapter explores the positive side of ADHD and how it can be used as a strength in entrepreneurship. It also identifies the key traits and skills that make people with ADHD successful entrepreneurs.
- **Chapter 4: How can ADHD be managed?** This chapter offers some practical tips and advice on how to manage the potential pitfalls of ADHD and avoid common mistakes that can derail your entrepreneurial journey. It also covers topics such as self-care, organization, support, balance, and learning.
- **Chapter 5: How can I become an entrepreneur?** This chapter guides you through the process of becoming an

entrepreneur with ADHD. It also provides some examples and resources to help you start, launch, and run your own business.

- **Chapter 6: Conclusion.** This chapter summarizes the main points of the book and provides some suggestions for further reading and action on ADHD and entrepreneurship.

The journey ahead is yours to claim. Embrace your ADHD, cultivate its strengths, strategically navigate its challenges, and step confidently onto the entrepreneurial path. You have what it takes. Your ADHD is not just a part of you; it is your distinct, powerful advantage.

II

Part Two

4

# The Authentic Heart: Cultivating Connectedness and Emotional Well-being in Neurodivergent Adults

*Section 1: Connectedness, Not Just Connection: The Neurodivergent Path to Belonging*

At the core of the human experience lies an intrinsic, fundamental need: the desire for belonging, for connection. This yearning to be seen, understood, and valued is universal, transcending neurotype. Yet, for neurodivergent adults, this pursuit of belonging often takes on a distinctly profound and nuanced form. They are not merely seeking superficial interactions or fleeting acquaintances; what they truly crave, and indeed thrive on, is **connectedness**.

Connectedness, in a psychological sense, refers to the deep, resonant feeling of belonging and being genuinely valued by others for one's authentic self. It's a foundational psychological need, as essential for survival and growth as food and water. When fostered, connectedness has a cascading positive impact on both physical and mental health, significantly reducing stress, bolstering immunity, elevating self-esteem, and cultivating a profound sense of happiness and contentment.

For neurodivergent adults, the quest for connectedness is imbued with particular significance. Their "different way of sensing, thinking, and learning" often translates into a unique internal world, one that can be a formidable source of power, unbounded creativity, and unconventional problem-solving. They frequently experience emotions with a vivid intensity, often possessing a profound capacity for empathy and an innate, heartfelt kindness. This depth of feeling drives a powerful desire to both offer and receive emotional security – a universal yearning, yet one they often express with unwavering sincerity. The neurodivergent adult has an inherent capacity to forge intensely meaningful relationships, giving themselves wholeheartedly and authentically. Does this sound familiar? For many, it resonates deeply.

However, this authentic and intense approach to relationships can also, paradoxically, be a source of vulnerability. In a society largely structured around neurotypical norms, neurodivergent individuals frequently encounter social exclusion, subtle microaggressions, overt rejection, or outright discrimination simply because their innate ways of being differ from the conventional. This systemic misunderstanding, as discussed in Chapter 2, can lead to painful experiences of isolation and alienation, making genuine connectedness an even more vital buffer against stigma's corrosive effects. True connectedness, therefore, acts as a sanctuary, allowing them to celebrate their unique strengths and talents, and crucially, to express their true, unmasked selves without fear of judgment.

The journey toward connectedness for neurodivergent adults is not without its distinct challenges. They may navigate inherent difficulties in conventional communication, struggle to interpret nuanced neurotypical social cues, or find traditional reciprocal conversation patterns baffling. Their needs and preferences regarding the quantity and quality of social interactions may diverge significantly from neurotypical expectations. For instance, the concept of a "social battery" – the finite energy available for social engagement – is particularly salient for many neurodivergent individuals, dictating a need for more downtime or quieter interactions. They may also encounter systemic barriers or a lack of accessible resources and opportunities that could otherwise facilitate authentic connection.

Consequently, cultivating connectedness for neurodivergent adults demands a multifaceted approach, requiring conscious awareness, genuine acceptance, and intentional adaptation from both themselves and others. It necessitates recognizing and respecting the profound diversity and inherent uniqueness of each individual's neurocognitive profile. It calls for the deliberate creation and sustained nurturing of environments that are not just tolerant, but actively inclusive, genuinely supportive, and deeply empowering for all neurotypes.

Fostering and Maintaining Connectedness: Practical Pathways

Navigating the social landscape as a neurodivergent adult requires a proactive and thoughtful approach. Here are expanded tips on fostering and maintaining authentic connectedness:

1. **Cultivate Radical Self-Awareness:**

- **Understand Your Social Needs:** Introspect to understand your optimal social 'dosage.' Do you thrive in small, intense groups or one-on-one? How much social interaction is energizing vs. draining? Recognize your "social battery" limits.
- **Identify Your Communication Style:** Understand how you naturally communicate (e.g., direct, literal, detail-oriented). Recognize common neurotypical communication patterns (e.g., implied meanings, indirectness) that might be challenging for you.
- **Set Clear Boundaries:** Learn to politely decline social engagements that exceed your capacity or don't align with your values. Communicate your needs clearly and kindly ("I need some quiet time to recharge"). This prevents burnout and fosters genuine respect.

1. **Embrace Authentic Unmasking:**

- **The Courage to Be Yourself:** The fear of judgment often leads to "masking" – suppressing natural behaviors and mimicking neurotypical social norms. While masking can be a survival mechanism, it drains energy and prevents genuine connection, as others are connecting with a persona, not your true self.
- **Gradual Disclosure:** You don't have to unmask all at once or to everyone. Choose safe spaces and trusted individuals

to gradually reveal more of your authentic self. Observe their reactions and build trust.

- **Communicate Your Neurotype (When Safe):** For those you trust, consider explaining your ADHD or neurodivergence. This provides context for your behaviors and communication style, fostering understanding rather than misinterpretation. Phrases like, "My brain works a bit differently, so sometimes I need things explained very literally," can be helpful.

1. **Seek Neurodivergent-Affirming Spaces and Communities:**

- **Online Communities:** Explore online forums, social media groups, and dedicated platforms for neurodivergent individuals. These can be invaluable for finding people who genuinely "get it," offering validation and practical advice.
- **Support Groups:** Local or virtual ADHD/autism support groups provide a safe environment for sharing experiences, learning coping strategies, and building camaraderie.
- **Special Interest Groups:** Engage in hobbies or interest-based groups where shared passion transcends neurotypical social norms. Many neurodivergent individuals find deep connection in highly specialized clubs (e.g., gaming, coding, specific crafts, niche literature groups).
- **Neurodivergent-Led Organizations:** Connect with organizations run by and for neurodivergent individuals, which often champion neurodiversity affirmation and provide inclusive spaces.

## 1. Educate Others (When Appropriate and Safe):

- **Provide Gentle Guidance:** Not everyone will understand neurodivergence intuitively. For those open to learning, patiently explain how your brain works or why you might react in certain ways.
- **Share Resources:** Direct curious friends or family to reputable articles, videos, or books that explain ADHD or neurodiversity in an accessible way.
- **Focus on Impact, Not Blame:** When communication breakdowns occur, focus on the impact ("When X happens, I feel Y") rather than assigning blame. This promotes understanding and problem-solving.

## 1. Prioritize Quality Over Quantity:

- **Deep Connections:** For many neurodivergent adults, a few deep, meaningful connections are far more fulfilling than a large network of superficial acquaintances. Invest your limited social energy where it truly counts.
- **Shared Understanding:** Seek out relationships where there's mutual respect for differences and a willingness to understand each other's unique perspectives.
- **Direct Communication:** Value relationships where direct, honest communication is appreciated, and where misunderstandings can be clarified without excessive subtext.

## 1. Respect Different Social Rhythms:

- **Acknowledge Varied Needs:** Understand that social

interaction doesn't always have to look like neurotypical
socializing (e.g., small talk, large parties). For some, a
shared quiet activity or a focused discussion is more
connecting.

- **Allow for Recharge Time:** For yourself and others. If
a friend needs to cancel plans last minute due to social
exhaustion, extend understanding, and expect the same in
return.
- **Flexible Socializing:** Explore alternative ways to connect,
such as virtual hangouts, shared online gaming, or even
asynchronous communication that reduces immediate
social pressure.

By embracing these strategies, neurodivergent adults can
actively cultivate an environment of authentic connectedness,
countering the effects of isolation and stigma, and ultimately
thriving within relationships that truly value their unique
perspectives and profound contributions.

*Section 2: The Emotional Lives of Neurodivergent Adults:
Intensity, Authenticity, and Regulation*

The emotional landscape of neurodivergent adults is often described as a vivid, high-definition panorama, experienced with
an intensity, complexity, and immediacy that can profoundly
differentiate it from neurotypical emotional experiences. This
isn't merely a subjective perception; neurobiological differences, particularly in brain regions associated with emotional
processing and regulation, often contribute to what can feel

like a perpetual "volume knob" turned up to eleven.

Neurodivergent adults may indeed be more prone to experiencing the extremes of emotional states, and in some contexts, may face heightened vulnerability to certain mood and anxiety disorders, or challenges in emotional stability, especially as they navigate the complexities of middle age and beyond. You might not be familiar with phrases like "loving-too-much syndrome" or "getting-too-needy syndrome," but for many neurodivergent individuals, these descriptors resonate deeply with their lived reality. The pain of a breakup, for instance, can linger with an enduring intensity, a profound grief that extends far beyond neurotypical recovery timelines. Yet, this emotional depth is not a weakness; it is the flip side of a remarkable capacity to love and seek connection in a fundamentally different, often far more authentic, way than what is frequently portrayed or practiced in mainstream neurotypical culture.

Emotions themselves are intricate psychological phenomena, encompassing subjective feelings, physiological responses (e.g., a racing heart), cognitive appraisals (how we interpret events), behavioral expressions (a smile, a tear), and complex social interactions. They serve critical functions: motivating us to act, signaling our needs, cementing our memories, and facilitating profound communication.

For neurodivergent adults, these emotional processes can be more intense, more varied, and sometimes more unpredictable. They may experience emotions with greater frequency, heightened strength, and rapid shifts. This heightened reactivity can be attributed to several factors, including:

- **Emotional Dysregulation:** Difficulty in managing emotional responses or keeping them within a tolerable range. This can lead to intense outbursts, prolonged emotional states, or an inability to calm down once upset.

- **Alexithymia:** A common co-occurring trait, not exclusive to neurodivergence, which describes difficulty identifying and describing one's own emotions. This can make it hard to understand *what* you're feeling, let alone *why* or *how* to manage it.
- **Heightened Sensory Processing:** Overwhelm from sensory input (lights, sounds, textures, smells) can directly trigger or exacerbate emotional responses, leading to meltdowns or shutdowns that are fundamentally emotional reactions to sensory overload.
- **Cognitive Rigidity (for some neurotypes):** Difficulty shifting focus or perspective can lead to getting "stuck" in a negative emotional loop.
- **Rejection Sensitive Dysphoria (RSD):** An intense emotional and physical pain response to perceived or actual rejection, criticism, or failure, disproportionate to the event. This can lead to extreme reactions or avoidance of situations where rejection is possible.

These emotional differences present both profound advantages and distinct challenges:

**Advantages:**

- **Deep Passion and Creativity:** Intense emotions can fuel incredible passion, driving individuals to pursue their interests with unparalleled dedication and inspiring remarkable creative output.
- **Profound Empathy and Compassion:** The ability to

feel deeply often translates into a powerful capacity for empathy, allowing neurodivergent individuals to connect with the struggles of others on a visceral level and respond with genuine compassion.

- **Authenticity and Honesty:** A strong internal compass often means a directness in emotional expression, a reduced capacity for pretense, and a profound value for honesty and loyalty in relationships. What you see is often what you get, which can foster deep trust.
- **Unconditional Love and Loyalty:** The "loving-too-much" syndrome, while sometimes painful, reflects an extraordinary capacity for deep, unconditional attachment and loyalty. For neurodivergent adults, love is often an unwavering commitment, a bond that endures beyond superficial shifts. They are often less bound by neurotypical "games" or social maneuvering in relationships, prioritizing genuine connection over performative affection.

**Disadvantages:**

- **Vulnerability to Overwhelm:** The intensity of emotions can quickly lead to emotional flooding, making it difficult to function or respond rationally.
- **Impulsivity and Reactivity:** Strong emotions can bypass logical processing, leading to impulsive decisions or reactive outbursts that are later regretted.
- **Misunderstanding and Judgment:** Neurotypical individuals may misinterpret intense or unconventional emotional expressions as overreactions, immaturity, or manipulation, leading to judgment, dismissal, or rejection.
- **Burnout:** The sheer energetic cost of constantly managing

intense emotions, especially when masking, can lead to severe emotional and physical exhaustion.

Therefore, navigating the emotional lives of neurodivergent adults necessitates a deep commitment to awareness, self-acceptance, and adaptive strategies from both the individual and their social circle. It demands recognizing and respecting the unique nuances of each person's emotional experience and fostering environments that are compassionate, supportive, and respectful of diverse emotional expressions.

Managing Emotions Effectively and Healthily: Strategies for Neurodivergent Adults

Cultivating emotional well-being is a dynamic process, requiring intentional strategies tailored to the neurodivergent experience.

1. **Develop Emotional Self-Awareness:**

- **Identify Triggers:** Pay attention to what situations, sensory inputs, or interactions consistently provoke strong emotional responses. Keep a journal to track patterns.
- **Recognize Early Warning Signs:** Learn to identify the subtle physical or cognitive cues (e.g., clenched jaw, racing thoughts, restlessness) that signal an emotional escalation before it becomes overwhelming.
- **Emotional Vocabulary Expansion:** If you struggle with alexithymia, start by using broad categories ("uncomfortable," "overwhelmed," "good") and gradually expand your emotional lexicon through resources like emotion wheels.

1. **Master Emotional Regulation Skills:**

- **Grounding Techniques:** When feeling overwhelmed, engage your senses to anchor yourself in the present moment:
- **5-4-3-2-1 Method:** Name 5 things you can see, 4 you can touch, 3 you can hear, 2 you can smell, 1 you can taste.
- **Tactile Input:** Use a weighted blanket, fidget toy, or soft fabric to provide calming sensory input.
- **Temperature Regulation:** Splash cold water on your face, hold an ice cube, or take a cool shower.
- **Deep Breathing Exercises:** Practice diaphragmatic breathing (breathing into your belly) to activate your parasympathetic nervous system, promoting calm. Techniques like box breathing (inhale 4, hold 4, exhale 4, hold 4) are effective.
- **Sensory Regulation Strategies:** Actively manage your sensory environment. Dim lights, use noise-canceling headphones, wear comfortable clothing, and take sensory breaks in quiet spaces.
- **Scheduled Breaks and Movement:** Integrate regular breaks, especially movement breaks, into your day to release pent-up energy and prevent emotional buildup.
- **Distraction and Redirection:** Learn to temporarily redirect your focus when emotions are too intense. Engage in a preferred hyperfocus activity, listen to music, or do something physically active.

1. **Learn to Identify and Articulate Emotions:**

- **"Name It to Tame It":** Even if you can only identify a

vague discomfort, putting a name to an emotion, however broad, begins the process of gaining control.

- **Use "I Feel" Statements:** Practice expressing your feelings directly, focusing on your internal experience rather than blaming others. "I feel overwhelmed when there's too much noise" is more effective than "You're making too much noise!"
- **Visual Aids:** Some neurodivergent individuals benefit from using charts or visual scales to express their emotional state to others if verbal articulation is difficult.

1. **Seek Neurodivergent-Affirming Professional Support:**

- **Therapy (CBT, DBT, Neurodivergent-Affirming):** Therapists trained in these modalities can provide invaluable tools for emotional regulation, distress tolerance, interpersonal effectiveness, and processing emotional experiences, particularly those related to neurodivergence and stigma.
- **ADHD Coaches:** Coaches can help develop practical strategies for managing emotional responses in daily life and in relationships.
- **Medication Review:** For severe emotional dysregulation, a healthcare professional can assess if medication (including ADHD medication or other psychotropics) could offer supportive relief.

1. **Communicate Emotional Needs and Boundaries:**

- **Educate Loved Ones:** For those you trust, explain *how*

your emotions work. "When I get overwhelmed, I need to step away for 10 minutes to reset, it's not personal."
- **Express Needs Directly:** Clearly state what you need when you're emotionally vulnerable, whether it's space, comfort, or a specific type of support.
- **Set Boundaries Around Emotional Labor:** Be mindful of not becoming an emotional sponge for others if it consistently drains your resources.

1. **Practice Self-Compassion and Acceptance:**

- **Release Shame:** Understand that your emotional intensity is a part of your neurodivergent wiring, not a flaw to be ashamed of.
- **Be Kind to Yourself:** During emotional surges or setbacks, practice self-kindness. Avoid harsh self-criticism. Remind yourself that you are doing your best with a uniquely wired brain.
- **Embrace Your Authenticity:** Recognize that your capacity for deep love, intense passion, and unwavering loyalty are remarkable strengths. While they may lead to more profound emotional experiences, they also enable unparalleled depth in your relationships and pursuits.

By integrating these strategies, neurodivergent adults can navigate their rich and intense emotional lives with greater skill and self-acceptance, fostering genuine connectedness and a profound sense of well-being, allowing their authentic heart to thrive.

# 5

# The Invisible Agony: DDD Parents Facing Divorce, Parental Alienation, and Hidden Emotional Distress

**Introduction: When the Heart and Brain Are in Crisis**

Losing a partner, and even more heartbreaking, witnessing the bond with one's child fray or be deliberately severed, ranks among the most devastating experiences any human being can go through. It is a trauma that shakes the very foundations of existence, plunging the individual into an abyss of grief, confusion, and despair. But for individuals living with **Dopamine Deficit Disorder (DDD)**, this ordeal can be exponentially more traumatic and complex. Their unique neurology, with its specificities in emotional regulation, rejection sensitivity, impulse control, and practical life management, amplifies every facet of this agony, often unseen by the world.

This chapter delves into the heart of this hidden suffering.

69

We will explore the specific challenges and profound pains encountered by DDD parents when faced with divorce and, even worse, parental alienation. The objective is to validate the traumatic nature of their experience, to dissect how DDD characteristics exacerbate this ordeal, and to propose concrete paths for healing, resilience, and reconnection, while acknowledging the systemic obstacles that make their journey even more arduous.

## Section 1: Validating the Traumatic Nature of Emotional and Systemic Distancing

The loss of a partner and the threat or reality of losing a child are major life events, ranked among the greatest stressors. For parents with DDD, these events trigger a cascade of amplified reactions, due to their neurobiological peculiarities.

### 1. Emotional Dysregulation (ARA): An Anchored Inner Storm

DDD often impairs the ability to regulate emotions, a phenomenon we have termed **Affective Reactivity Amplification (ARA)** in Chapter 4. This means that individuals with DDD can experience more intense, frequent, and prolonged emotional reactions than others. Faced with the shock, anger, sadness, guilt, and overwhelming loneliness that come with losing a partner and a child, this dysregulation is a true inner storm.

- **Amplified Impact:** Where others might feel sadness, the DDD parent can plunge into an abyssal despair. Anger can become uncontrollable rage. Confusion transforms into a paralyzing mental fog. This intensity makes processing grief and loss exponentially more difficult. The brain, already in "dopaminergic emergency" (Chapter 5) to manage daily life, is overwhelmed by the trauma.

- **Practical Consequences:** This ARA can make it difficult to express emotions appropriately, leading to misunderstandings, exacerbated conflicts with the ex-partner (which can be used against the DDD parent in legal proceedings), or increased social isolation if those around them do not understand these intense reactions. Studies show that emotional dysregulation is a central characteristic of ADHD/DDD, affecting up to **50% to 70% of affected adults**, making the management of personal crises like divorce particularly difficult.

## 2. Rejection Sensitive Dysphoria (RSD): The Wound of Rejection Multiplied by Ten

DDD is often accompanied by **Rejection Sensitive Dysphoria (RSD)**, an emotionally and physically disproportionate response to the perception or experience of rejection, criticism, or failure (as discussed in Chapter 4). The loss of a partner and the alienation of a child are the ultimate triggers for RSD.

- **Amplified Impact:** The feeling of rejection, betrayal, and abandonment is experienced with unbearable psychological pain, often described as physical pain. Every sign of disinterest from the ex-partner, every cold word from the manipulated child, is a poisoned arrow that strikes directly at this vulnerability.

- **Practical Consequences:** RSD makes it extremely difficult to cope with rejection, to trust again, to seek support (for fear of further rejection), or to form new relationships. It can lead to social withdrawal, hyper-vigilance in interactions, and an inability to defend oneself effectively for fear of confrontation and additional rejection. Research estimates that RSD affects between **30% and 50% of individuals with ADHD/DDD clinically significantly**, making this experience a major risk factor for intense psychological distress during a breakup.

### 3. Impulsivity (PUR): Hasty Decisions in Chaos

DDD reduces the ability to control impulses, a phenomenon we have termed **Phenotype of Urgency for Reward (PUR)** (Chapter 4). Under the immense stress of a breakup and parental alienation, this impulsivity can manifest devastatingly.

- **Amplified Impact:** The DDD parent may act spontaneously or rashly under the influence of frustration, anxiety, or anger. This can result in verbal outbursts, hasty financial decisions, or behaviors that, while expressing deep pain, can be misinterpreted and used against them in a legal context.
- **Practical Consequences:** Impulsivity can make it difficult to avoid risky behaviors, such as substance abuse (an attempt at self-medication to manage emotional pain

and dopaminergic deficit, as seen in Chapter 10), self-harm, or confrontations that can harm the legal situation or the relationship with the child. Studies show that individuals with ADHD/DDD have a **two to three times higher risk of developing substance use disorders** than the general population, a risk that increases significantly during periods of intense stress and trauma.

## 4. Inattention and Executive Function Deficits (IMA, TAMD, VTO): Practical Chaos

DDD impairs the ability to maintain attention (IMA), manage working memory (TAMD), and organize/initiate tasks (VTO) (Chapter 4). These challenges become major obstacles when facing the practical and administrative demands of divorce and parental alienation.

- **Amplified Impact:** Managing legal aspects (deadlines, complex documents), financial issues (budgeting, tracking payments), or even daily household chores becomes an insurmountable mountain. The DDD parent may forget crucial appointments, misplace important papers, or struggle to follow their lawyer's instructions.
- **Practical Consequences:** This disorganization can lead to legal delays, financial losses, and an inability to maintain a stable environment for oneself, which can be perceived negatively by authorities or the ex-partner, reinforcing the argument that the parent is "irresponsible" or "incapable," even if that is not the case. Executive function deficits are at the heart of ADHD/DDD and impact almost all

areas of life, making the management of a complex crisis particularly overwhelming.


## 5. Discrimination and Systemic Injustice: The Fight Against Invisible Walls

DDD, being an invisible disability, exposes parents to insidious discrimination from various systems.

- **The Legal System:** Courts, often untrained in the nuances of DDD, may interpret manifestations of the disorder (ARA as "instability," impulsivity as "irresponsibility," VTO as "lack of commitment") punitively. Non-specialized lawyers may not know how to effectively defend a DDD client. Parents may struggle to defend their rights, access resources, or maintain fair contact with their child. Studies and reports from neurodivergent rights organizations have documented cases where ADHD/DDD is used as an argument to limit custody or visitation rights, even in the absence of real danger to the child.
- **Society and Surroundings:** The DDD parent may face stigma, prejudice, or harassment from their social circle, who do not understand the complexity of their situation.
- **The Ex-Partner and Child:** In cases of parental alienation, the ex-partner may deliberately exploit the DDD symptoms of the alienated parent (for example, by highlighting their disorganization or intense emotional reactions) to discredit them with the child and the judicial system. The manipulated child may internalize these prejudices, rejecting the parent based on characteristics

related to their DDD.

- **Practical Consequences:** This discrimination can have devastating consequences on the DDD parent's life, leading to loss of custody, social isolation, and increased psychological distress. The system, supposedly just, becomes a new "incentive trap" (Chapter 10) that disadvantages the neurodivergent parent.

*Section 2: Letting Go by Embracing Harsh Reality: Neuro-Affirming Healing Strategies*

Losing a partner and watching one's child drift away is a heartbreaking and life-changing event. For DDD parents, the pain is tenfold, an emotional hemorrhage that persists long after the other has left. However, this reality, however harsh, is not an end. It is possible to heal, rebuild, and thrive again. Here are concrete strategies, adapted to the specificities of the DDD brain, for navigating this process.

## 1. Accepting the Reality of Loss, Not Guilt:

- **The Harsh Reality:** "Your ex stopped loving you." This is a brutal truth, but necessary to face and accept. Their feelings cannot be changed. Letting go of their decision is an act of respect for them and liberation for you. Understand that their love was not meant for you, and that you deserve someone who loves you unconditionally.

- **Neuro-Affirming Strategy:** For a brain with RSD, this acceptance is an immense challenge. Focus on validating your own intrinsic worth, regardless of the ex-partner's approval. Use positive affirmations that strengthen your self-esteem.

## 2. Honoring Your Unique Grieving Process:

- **The Compassionate Reality:** "You don't have to stop loving them at the same time." You cannot force yourself to stop feeling what you feel or erase the memories you shared. You must acknowledge and express your love in healthy ways, without letting it consume you. Your love was genuine and beautiful, and you are capable of loving again.
- **Neuro-Affirming Strategy:** DDD parents may experience grief with different intensity and duration (ARA). Allow yourself to feel your emotions fully without judgment. Acceptance and Commitment Therapy (ACT) can help you navigate this pain without clinging to it dysfunctionally. Writing, art, or intense physical exercise (DRC) can be powerful outlets for emotional release.

## 3. Cultivating an Attitude of Strength and Radical Honesty:

- **The Positive Reality:** Constantly remind yourself of your good qualities and achievements. Focus on the future instead of dwelling on the past.

- **Neuro-Affirming Strategy:** For brains with VTO and DFR, focusing on the future is difficult. Break down future goals into concrete, immediately rewarding micro-steps. Celebrate every small victory. Create a "vision board" to make the future more tangible and motivating. Gratitude for your strengths (Chapter 3) and past successes can counteract the tendency for negative rumination.

## 4. Reclaiming Control of Your Emotional Response:

- **The Empowering Reality:** "You get to decide what to feel and what you are most comfortable with." Do not let your emotions overwhelm you or dictate your actions. Learn to regulate and manage your emotions in appropriate ways. Your emotions are valid and important, and you can choose how to react.
- **Neuro-Affirming Strategy:** For managing ARA and PUR, this involves specific techniques:
- **The "10-Second Pause":** Before reacting impulsively, force yourself to pause.
- **Emotional Regulation Techniques (DBT):** Learn skills such as distress tolerance (distraction, self-soothing), emotional regulation (checking the facts, acting opposite), and interpersonal effectiveness.
- **Trigger Identification:** Understand what triggers your intense reactions and develop action plans to avoid or manage them.

## 5. The Ultimate Act of Love: Freeing the Other to Free Yourself:

- **The Liberating Reality:** "If you truly love someone, you also choose for them to go if they don't feel the same way." Do not hold on to someone who does not want to be with you or beg for their attention. Release them and wish them well. Letting go is an act of love, and it sets you free. "Go and forget about me. Because I can't stop loving you yet, no matter how hard I try."
- **Neuro-Affirming Strategy:** For brains with DFR and PUR, perseverance can turn into obsession. Radical acceptance is key. Focus on what is within your control (your own actions and reactions), not on the other's actions. Mindfulness meditation can help cultivate emotional detachment without suppression.

## 6. Surviving and Thriving: Your Unaltered Potential:

- **The Hopeful Reality:** "You can survive this, and you can thrive again." You are not alone, and you are not hopeless. You are a strong and resilient person, and you have a lot to offer yourself and others. You are a DDD parent who is left behind, but you are also so much more. Do not give up on yourself or your life because of this loss. Heal yourself and rebuild your life. Surviving is possible, and thriving is attainable.
- **Neuro-Affirming Strategy:** Activate your neuroplastic-

ity (Chapter 9) to wire new positive pathways. Set new goals aligned with your passions (Chapter 3). Surround yourself with a supportive community (Chapter 14) that validates your experience and celebrates your strengths.

**Essential Practical Tips (Reaffirmation and Expansion of "Useless Advice"):**

Generic advice can seem "useless" for a DDD brain. Here's how to make it concrete and effective:

1. **Seek Specialized and Neuro-Affirming Professional Help:**

- **Why it's Crucial:** A therapist specializing in DDD, grief, and trauma is essential. They will understand how your IMA, ARA, and PUR impact your grieving process and help you develop tailored strategies. They can also address underlying comorbidities (anxiety, depression, SUD) in an integrated way. Do not settle for a general therapist; seek an expert in neurodiversity.
- **Concrete Action:** Ask for recommendations from DDD associations. During the first contact, explicitly ask about their experience with DDD and trauma/grief.

1. **Join a Neurodivergent Support Group:**

- **Why it's Crucial:** Connecting with other DDD parents who have gone through similar situations offers unique validation and practical advice that only peers can provide.

It's a safe space to share without judgment.

- **Concrete Action:** Look for online or in-person support groups specifically for DDD parents or divorced neurodivergent adults. Organizations like CHADD, ADDA, or local groups can be a starting point.

1. **Prioritize Radical and Structured Self-Care:**

- **Why it's Crucial:** Your physical and mental health are your foundation. For a DDD brain, this requires conscious structure.
- **Concrete Action:**
- **Nutrition:** Prepare simple, nutritious meals in advance (meal prep). Use meal delivery services if necessary.
- **Sleep:** Establish a strict bedtime routine, even if falling asleep is difficult (IMA, DRC). Avoid screens before bed.
- **Exercise:** Incorporate physical activities you enjoy (DRC) – even short walks or dance sessions. Movement releases dopamine and helps regulate emotions.
- **Pleasure and Accomplishment:** Consciously plan activities that bring you joy and a sense of accomplishment, however small (PUR, DFR).

1. **Maintain Strategic and Safe Contact with Your Child:**

- **Why it's Crucial:** Maintaining a positive and loving bond despite distance and obstacles is vital for the child and for your own healing.
- **Concrete Action:**
- **Consistency:** Even if visits are limited, be unfailingly reliable (VTO).

- **Adapted Communication:** Use visual aids, short and clear messages. Avoid conflict topics. Focus on unconditional love.
- **Documentation:** Keep accurate records of all contact attempts and communications, useful in legal proceedings.

1. **Seek Specialized Legal Advice:**

- **Why it's Crucial:** The legal system is a major "incentive trap" for DDD parents. A lawyer specializing in family law *and* familiar with DDD is essential to protect your rights and navigate complexities.
- **Concrete Action:** Look for lawyers who have experience with neurodivergent clients. Be prepared to provide detailed information about your DDD (with the help of your therapist) so your lawyer can defend you effectively. Ask for written instructions and reminders for deadlines.

*Section 3: The Horrors of Neurotypical Ghosting and Its Devastating Effects on DDD Victims*

"Ghosting" – a term all too familiar in modern relationships – refers to the abrupt disappearance and sudden silence of one person, leaving the other in a state of confusion, pain, and unanswered questions. For most, it's an unpleasant experience. But for individuals with DDD, ghosting can be much more than a minor emotional setback; it can be a devastating blow, amplifying already existing vulnerabilities and undermining an often-fragile sense of self.

## 1. The Amplified Struggle with Rejection Sensitive Dysphoria (RSD):

Ghosting is the ultimate trigger for **Rejection Sensitive Dysphoria (RSD)**, a common and deeply painful experience for individuals with DDD. RSD is an emotional and physical reaction of extreme intensity to the perception or reality of rejection or criticism. When someone with DDD is "ghosted," this emotional rollercoaster escalates rapidly. The brain is flooded with questions: "What did I do wrong? Why don't they like me? Am I unlovable?" The pain is physical, the feeling of being broken is complete.

- **Empirical Evidence:** RSD is a very frequent comorbidity of ADHD/DDD, with studies suggesting that up to **50% of individuals with ADHD/DDD experience clinically significant RSD**. Ghosting, by its ambiguous nature and lack of closure, is the perfect catalyst for this pain, leaving the victim without explanation to rationalize or process the situation.

## 2. Social Cues and Misinterpretations (IMA, TAMD):

Individuals with DDD often struggle to accurately read and interpret subtle social cues, a difficulty linked to **Inattention Modulation Instability (IMA)** and **Delayed Access to Dynamic Memory (TAMD)**. They may misinterpret a lack of communication as disinterest or rejection. When ghosting occurs, the DDD brain, in its quest for meaning and closure, replays every interaction, analyzing every word, every gesture, searching for the slightest clue. This hyper-focus on past details, combined with the difficulty of remembering interactions precisely (TAMD), can lead to intense self-blame and a profound feeling of inadequacy.

## 3. Devastated Self-Esteem:

Ghosting reinforces negative self-perceptions. Individuals with DDD often already battle feelings of being "different," "inadequate," or "misunderstood" due to their neurodivergent traits. Ghosting amplifies these insecurities, causing them to question their worthiness of love and connection. It is a direct attack on an already fragile self-esteem.

## 4. The Digital Incentive Trap:

Ghosting is facilitated by the nature of modern digital communication, which offers "low friction" for avoidance. There is no direct confrontation, no difficult conversation. For the "ghoster," it's a quick solution (a dopamine "hit" from conflict avoidance). But for the DDD victim, who craves clarity and closure (DFR), it's torture. The lack of response is an incentive for endless rumination.

## You Are Not Alone: Finding Inner Closure

It is crucial to remember that you are not alone in this experience. Many people – neurotypical and neurodivergent – have faced ghosting. It is never a reflection of your value as a person; it is always a reflection of the other person's inability to communicate honestly and with respect.

While closure from the other party may never come, you can give yourself the closure you deserve. This is an act of self-compassion and empowerment:

- **Acknowledge and Validate Your Feelings (ARA):** Allow yourself to feel the hurt, disappointment, anger, and confusion. Do not suppress these emotions. Let them pass through, even if they are intense. Writing, talking to a trusted friend, or art can be healthy outlets.

- **Release Blame:** Understand that ghosting is about the other person's limitations (their fear of conflict, their lack of emotional maturity), not about your shortcomings. You are not responsible for their actions.

- **Focus on Radical Self-Care (IMA, DRC):** Engage in activities that nourish your physical and mental well-being. Physical exercise (DRC), mindfulness, a healthy diet, and sufficient sleep are essential anchors when the world feels chaotic. These practical actions help regulate your dopaminergic system.

- **Seek Specialized Support:** Reach out to trusted friends, family members, or a therapist specializing in DDD and relational trauma. They can offer empathetic perspective and tools to navigate this pain.

- **Create Your Own Closure:** Since the other person won't provide it, create it for yourself. This may involve writing a letter you'll never send, creating a symbolic "letting go" ritual, or simply consciously deciding that this story is over and you deserve to move forward.

- **Reaffirm Your Worth:** Constantly remind yourself that

you deserve respect, kindness, and honest communication, even when others fail to provide them. Your worth is intrinsic and unchangeable.

## Conclusion: From Agony to Resilience – The DDD Parent's Journey

The path of a DDD parent facing divorce and parental alienation is fraught with unique challenges, amplified by neurological peculiarities often misunderstood by the systems meant to support them. The emotional agony is profound, the struggle against stigma and injustice is exhausting, and the phenomenon of ghosting adds an insidious layer of pain.

However, this chapter is not a litany of despair. It is a call for recognition, validation, and action. By understanding the amplified mechanisms of pain – from ARA to RSD, from IMA to impulsivity – we can finally offer healing strategies that are truly adapted. By recognizing systemic pitfalls, we can advocate for changes that protect DDD parents.

The resilience of DDD parents is immense. Their capacity to love deeply, their creativity in finding solutions, and their determination to maintain a bond with their children, even in the face of adversity, are testaments to their strength. By arming themselves with knowledge, seeking specialized support, and engaging in radical self-care strategies, DDD parents can not only survive these ordeals but also emerge stronger, more conscious, and more fulfilled. The path is arduous, but the promise of a rebuilt life, where love and well-being can once again flourish, is within reach for those who dare to embrace their reality and fight for their dignity.

6

# Mastering the Emotional Symphony: Navigating and Transforming Emotional Neurodivergence with DDD

**I**ntroduction: The Unseen Orchestra of Feelings

Emotional neurodivergence is a profound and often misunderstood aspect of human experience, describing how some individuals perceive, process, and express emotions in ways that deviate from typical norms. It is not a flaw, but a distinct way of being, often stemming from neurobiological differences inherent in conditions such as autism, trauma, personality variations, and crucially, **Dopamine Deficit Disorder (DDD)**. For those with DDD, this neurodivergence can manifest as a heightened emotional landscape – a rich, vibrant, and sometimes overwhelming "symphony" of feelings. We may experience emotions more intensely, possess a profound sensitivity to external and internal stimuli, exhibit heightened empathy, or demonstrate a remarkable capacity for creative expression.

However, this amplified emotional world also presents unique challenges. A common struggle is **emotional dysregulation**, a term that describes the difficulty in managing one's emotions in ways deemed appropriate or effective for a given situation. For individuals with DDD, emotional dysregulation is not merely a "lack of control"; it is often a direct consequence of the **Affective Reactivity Amplification (ARA)** and **Phenotype of Urgency for Reward (PUR)** as discussed in Chapter 4, where the brain's unique wiring impacts the speed and intensity of emotional responses and the drive for immediate emotional relief. This can lead to a cascade of difficulties, including impulsivity, frustration, anxiety, depression, withdrawal, or even self-harm, and profoundly impact our relationships. Others, operating from a neurotypical framework, may struggle to understand or accept our emotional expressions, leading to isolation and feelings of invalidation.

This chapter is an invitation to explore a transformative path: not to "tame" our emotional neurodivergence as if it were a wild beast to be subdued, but to **master** its intricacies. It is about understanding the unique rhythms of our emotional symphony, learning to conduct its diverse instruments, and ultimately, harnessing its power for good. We will delve into seven interconnected steps designed to help individuals with DDD embrace their emotional depth, navigate challenges with greater skill, and cultivate a life rich in authentic feeling and resilient action. By learning to harmonize our feelings with our actions, we can reclaim our emotional sovereignty and transform perceived weaknesses into profound strengths.

*Section 1: Recognizing and Naming Your Emotions: Tuning into Your Inner Landscape*

The first and foundational step in mastering your emotional neurodivergence is to develop a keen awareness of what you are feeling and, crucially, why. For individuals with DDD, this initial step can be particularly challenging due to the **Inattention Modulation Instability (IMA)** and **Delayed Access to Dynamic Memory (TAMD)**, which can make it difficult to focus on internal states or recall the precise triggers of past emotional experiences. Our brains, constantly seeking external novelty (as per the **Drive for Novelty and Risk (DFR)**, Chapter 4), may struggle to settle into the quiet introspection required to pinpoint elusive feelings.

- **The Challenge for DDD:** Imagine trying to hear a single instrument in a chaotic orchestra when your attention is constantly being pulled to other sounds, or when you can't quite recall the melody that preceded the current discord. This is similar to the difficulty many DDD individuals face in interoception — the ability to perceive internal bodily states, including emotions. The fast-paced, often fragmented internal experience can make it hard to pause, identify, and label emotions accurately. Furthermore, the tendency to jump from one thought to another or the difficulty in sustained mental effort (IMA) can hinder the consistent practice needed for emotional self-awareness.

- **Actionable Strategies for DDD:**
- **Emotion Journaling (Low-Demand Format):** Instead of lengthy prose, consider short, bullet-point entries. Use templates with prompts like "Today I felt X when Y happened." Integrate visual elements like emojis or color-coding. Use a voice-to-text app if writing is a barrier. The goal is consistency over perfection.
- **Mood Trackers & Apps (Visual & Gamified):** Leverage visual and gamified apps like Mood Meter, Daylio, or Bearable. These external memory aids help overcome TAMD by creating a tangible record of emotional patterns and triggers over time. Their interactive nature can also appeal to the DFR, making tracking less tedious.
- **Intensity Scales:** Use a simple 1-10 scale to rate the intensity of emotions. This provides a concrete, quantitative measure that can be easier for analytical DDD brains to grasp than abstract emotional nuances.
- **"What's In My Body?" Scan:** Beyond just naming emotions, practice checking in with physical sensations. Does anxiety feel like tightness in your chest? Does anger feel hot? This anchors the emotional experience to tangible bodily cues, which can be more accessible than purely abstract feelings for some DDD individuals.
- **Connection to DDD Mastery:** By consistently documenting and reflecting on your emotional states, you begin to identify patterns and trends, externalizing your internal experience. This process bypasses the challenges of IMA and TAMD by providing a structured, often visual, record that helps you build a more robust "emotional memory." It's like building an external database of your internal

symphony, allowing you to better understand its themes and variations. This enhanced self-awareness is the first step towards truly conducting your emotional life.

## Section 2: Validating Your Emotions: The Anchor of Acceptance

The second crucial step is to wholeheartedly accept and respect your emotions as valid and important, regardless of their intensity or their perceived "appropriateness" within a neurotypical framework. For individuals with DDD, this step is profoundly challenging due to **Rejection Sensitive Dysphoria (RSD)** and years of internalized shame, where intense or "different" emotional responses may have been criticized or misunderstood. We may have been told, explicitly or implicitly, that our feelings are "too much," "irrational," or "wrong."

- **The Challenge for DDD:** Imagine being told your favorite musical instrument plays too loudly or off-key, simply because others prefer a quieter, more predictable sound. This can lead to deep-seated shame and guilt about our emotional experiences. When RSD is activated, the internal critic amplifies, telling us we are fundamentally flawed for feeling what we feel. This can create a vicious cycle: intense emotion triggers shame, leading to suppression, which then makes emotional regulation even harder (ARA). Validation is about breaking this cycle.

- **Actionable Strategies for DDD:**
- **Neuro-Affirming Affirmations:** Develop personalized affirmations that directly counter past invalidation. Examples: "My feelings are valid, no matter how intense they are," "It's okay to feel deeply," "My emotional sensitivity is a strength, not a weakness." Write them down, say them aloud, or record them as audio reminders.
- **Mindful Self-Compassion Breaks:** When an intense emotion arises, acknowledge it without judgment. Place a hand over your heart, say to yourself, "This is a moment of suffering. Suffering is a part of life. May I be kind to myself in this moment." This simple act helps activate the parasympathetic nervous system, countering the fight-or-flight response often triggered by RSD.
- **Connecting with Neurodivergent Communities:** Sharing your emotional experiences within a community of other neurodivergent individuals can be incredibly validating. Hearing others express similar feelings can dismantle the belief that you are uniquely flawed. This external validation acts as a powerful antidote to RSD.
- **Creating an "Emotional Sanctuary":** Designate a physical or mental space where you allow yourself to feel any emotion without judgment. This could be a specific corner of a room, a journal, or a guided visualization. This ritual helps reinforce the message that your emotions are safe and acceptable.
- **Connection to DDD Mastery:** Validation directly addresses the core wounds of RSD and internalized shame. By actively accepting your emotions, you reduce the internal resistance that fuels emotional dysregulation. This step is about integrating your emotional self, recognizing

that your unique emotional "tuning" is neither wrong nor bad. It's about developing unconditional positive regard for your internal experience, a crucial step toward building resilience and self-worth.

## Section 3: Expressing Your Emotions: Creative Release and Authentic Communication

The third step involves finding healthy and constructive ways to communicate your emotions, both to yourself and to others. For individuals with DDD, who may experience intense internal states (ARA) and struggle with verbal self-regulation (PUR) in high-emotion situations, traditional verbal expression can feel daunting or lead to misunderstandings. Creative outlets and structured communication tools offer powerful alternatives.

- **The Challenge for DDD:** Imagine a powerful melody trapped inside, unable to find its way out through words. This can lead to emotional backlog, where suppressed feelings build up until they burst forth impulsively or turn inward, leading to anxiety or depression. The fear of being misunderstood, judged, or triggering RSD can also lead to avoidance of emotional expression.
- **Actionable Strategies for DDD:**
- **Creative Outlets (Leveraging DFR):** Channeling emotions into something meaningful and beautiful can be immensely therapeutic. This taps into the **Drive for**

**Novelty and Risk (DFR)** and the pursuit of engagement.

- **Visual Journaling:** Combine words with drawings, collages, or doodles to express feelings that words alone cannot capture. No artistic skill required.
- **Music:** Create playlists that match your moods, or try composing simple melodies or lyrics. Listening to music can also be a powerful way to process emotions (DRC - Dopaminergic Reward Circuit stimulation).
- **Movement & Dance:** Physical expression can release stored emotional energy. Improvised dance, even alone in your living room, can be incredibly liberating.
- **Digital Art/Design:** For those with a visual-spatial strength, digital platforms can offer a low-friction way to create and express.
- **Assertive Communication Skills (Scripting for PUR):**
- **"I-Statements":** Practice using phrases like "I feel [emotion] when [situation] because [need/impact]." This focuses on your experience rather than blaming the other person. Example: "I feel frustrated when plans change last minute because it disrupts my routine and I need predictability."
- **Active Listening (External Anchor):** When others express their emotions, consciously focus on understanding their perspective before formulating your response. This provides an external anchor, helping to slow down impulsive reactions.
- **Nonviolent Communication (NVC) Framework:** Learn the basic structure of NVC (Observation, Feeling, Need, Request). This provides a clear, empathetic framework for expressing your needs and emotions, especially useful for managing intense emotional discussions where PUR might otherwise derail you.

- **Pre-scripting Difficult Conversations:** For high-stakes emotional conversations, write down what you want to say beforehand. Practice it aloud. This can help manage impulsivity (PUR) and ensure clarity.
- **Connection to DDD Mastery:** Expressing emotions in healthy ways releases tension, prevents emotional backlog, and builds authentic connections. Creative outlets provide a neurodivergent-friendly "flow state" where emotions can be processed without the demands of direct verbalization. Structured communication tools offer scaffolding for verbal expression, helping to bypass the challenges of impulsivity and ensuring that your powerful emotional messages are received, not just reacted to. This step is about translating your inner symphony into forms that can be understood and shared.

*Section 4: Regulating Your Emotions: Dopaminergic Strategies for Stability*

The fourth step focuses on employing coping strategies and tools to modulate the intensity and duration of your emotions. For individuals with DDD, whose **Affective Reactivity Amplification (ARA)** means emotions can surge quickly and intensely, and whose **Dopaminergic Reward Circuit (DRC)** is constantly seeking stimulation, generic relaxation techniques often fall short. We need strategies that work with, rather than against, our unique neurological wiring.

- **The Challenge for DDD:** When an intense emotion strikes, the DDD brain can feel hijacked, spiraling rapidly into overwhelm (ARA). The natural inclination for some might be to seek immediate relief through less healthy impulses (PUR). Sustaining attention on calming techniques can also be difficult (IMA).
- **Actionable Strategies for DDD:**
- **Short, Focused Breathing Exercises:** Instead of long meditations, try brief, impactful breathing exercises. The "4-7-8" technique (inhale 4, hold 7, exhale 8) for a few repetitions can rapidly activate the parasympathetic nervous system. Use a timer or an app to provide external structure (VTO).
- **Targeted Physical Activity (DRC Activation):** Movement is a powerful regulator. For DDD, this means engaging in activities that provide a quick dopamine hit and physical release. This can be a short burst of jumping jacks, a brisk walk, dancing to upbeat music, or even simply shaking out your limbs. The key is active engagement that aligns with the **Dopaminergic Reward Circuit (DRC)**, making it more likely to be initiated and sustained.
- **Sensory Grounding Techniques:** When overwhelmed, engage your senses.
- **Sight:** Focus on 5 things you can see (colors, shapes).
- **Sound:** Identify 4 sounds you can hear (ticking clock, distant traffic).
- **Touch:** Feel 3 things (texture of your clothing, temperature of your skin).
- **Smell:** Notice 2 things you can smell.
- Taste: Identify 1 thing you can taste.
- This shifts focus from overwhelming internal states (IMA)

to the external present.

- **"Dopamine-Boosting" Distractions (Engaging Novelty):** While prolonged avoidance is not healthy, short, engaging distractions can provide a temporary reprieve to reset. This taps into the **Drive for Novelty and Risk (DFR)**. This could be a quick game, a challenging puzzle, a new captivating video, or a short, intense hobby that grabs your attention. The key is to choose activities that are genuinely engaging for *your* brain, not just generic suggestions.

- **Scheduled "Worry Time":** If rumination is a problem, schedule a specific 15-minute slot each day for "worry time." If a worry comes up outside this slot, note it down and tell yourself you'll deal with it later. This provides a structured container, appealing to the DDD brain's need for external organization (VTO).

- **Connection to DDD Mastery:** Regulating emotions for DDD involves understanding that intensity is a baseline, and finding strategies that effectively calm the nervous system and manage dopamine levels. These techniques are not about suppressing emotions, but about creating space between the feeling and the reaction, allowing for more intentional responses. By proactively employing these dopaminergic strategies, you gain greater control and stability over your emotional landscape, turning overwhelm into manageable energy.

## Section 5: Transforming Your Emotions: Rewiring the Brain for Growth

The fifth step moves beyond managing emotions in the moment to actively transforming their impact, leveraging cognitive strategies to change the way you think about and react to them. For the DDD brain, which can get stuck in negative thought loops (IMA, TAMD) or struggle with initiating complex problem-solving (VTO), this requires intentional reframing and structured approaches to neuroplasticity.

- **The Challenge for DDD:** Our brains are wired for efficiency, and negative thought patterns, once established, can become habitual. The constant "noise" of internal thoughts can make it difficult to intentionally shift perspective (IMA). When faced with emotionally charged challenges, the executive function deficits (VTO) can make it hard to break down problems and formulate effective solutions, leading to feelings of overwhelm and helplessness.
- **Actionable Strategies for DDD:**
- **Cognitive Reframing (Leveraging DFR for New Perspectives):** This involves consciously challenging negative thoughts and reinterpreting situations in a more constructive light. For DDD, it's about making this process engaging and "novel" enough to capture attention (DFR).
- **"Thought Detective" Worksheets:** Use structured worksheets to identify a negative thought, gather evidence for and against it, and then formulate a more balanced thought. This provides a concrete framework, appealing to the

DDD need for external organization (VTO).

- **Gratitude Practice (Specific and Novel):** Instead of a generic gratitude list, try to find *novel* things to be grateful for each day, or focus on specific details (e.g., "I'm grateful for the exact shade of blue in the sky today," rather than "I'm grateful for the sky"). This engages the DFR and makes the practice more sustainable.

- **Humor as a Cognitive Shift:** Actively seek out humor in situations, even difficult ones. Laughter is a powerful physiological and psychological disruptor of negative emotional states and can provide a quick, engaging cognitive shift.

- **Problem-Solving Techniques (Breaking Down VTO Barriers):**

- **The "Brain Dump" and Categorization:** When overwhelmed by a problem that triggers intense emotion, do a complete brain dump of every related thought and task. Then, categorize them into small, manageable chunks. This overcomes the "blank page paralysis" of VTO.

- **The "If-Then" Planning:** For known triggers or recurring emotional challenges, create "if-then" plans: "IF [trigger happens], THEN I will [specific, pre-determined action]." This pre-loads the response, bypassing the need for real-time decision-making when emotions are high (PUR, VTO).

- **Focus on the "Next Small Step":** Instead of trying to solve the entire problem, identify only the very next tiny action you can take. This makes initiation much easier, leveraging the principle of the **Drive for Routine and Completion (DRC)**, even if the routine is just one small step.

- **Connection to DDD Mastery:** Transforming emotions is about actively shaping your neuroplasticity. By consciously reframing thoughts and systematically approaching problems, you are literally rewiring your brain to respond differently. This process moves beyond merely reacting to your emotional symphony; it teaches you to compose new, more empowering melodies for your life, turning challenges into opportunities for profound growth.

## Section 6: Recognizing Your "Emotional Children": Healing Past Wounds

The sixth step invites a deeper exploration into the origins and influences of your emotions, particularly those intense, seemingly irrational, or persistent feelings that may stem from past experiences. For individuals with DDD, who may have experienced a lifetime of misunderstandings, criticisms, and inconsistencies due to their neurodivergence, this "inner child" work is crucial for healing deep-seated wounds that fuel current emotional dysregulation (ARA, RSD).

- **The Challenge for DDD:** Growing up with undiagnosed or unsupported DDD often means experiencing chronic invalidation, shame, and a sense of "not fitting in." We may have been labeled "lazy," "disorganized," or "too emotional," leading to an accumulation of trauma. These past experiences can manifest as "emotional children"

– younger parts of ourselves that carry unmet needs, fears, and unresolved pain. When current situations trigger these old wounds, the emotional response can be disproportionate because it's not just the current event but a lifetime of similar experiences coming to the surface, amplified by RSD.

- **Actionable Strategies for DDD:**
- **Inner Child Journaling/Dialogue:** Dedicate time to writing letters to your younger self, asking what they needed, what they felt, and what they would like you to know now. You can also write from the perspective of your "emotional child," giving voice to their pain. This externalizes internal dialogue, making it more manageable for the DDD brain (IMA, VTO).
- **Guided Meditations for Inner Child Work:** Many guided meditations specifically focus on connecting with and nurturing your inner child. These can provide structure and reduce the mental effort required for this deep work.
- **Attachment Theory in a DDD Context:** Understand how your early relationships, particularly if marked by inconsistency or misunderstanding (common for neuro-divergent children with neurotypical caregivers), shaped your attachment style (secure, anxious, avoidant, fearful). Recognize how these patterns influence your current relationships and emotional responses. This provides a cognitive framework for understanding deep-seated emotional patterns.
- **Reparenting Yourself:** Actively practice providing your "emotional children" with the compassion, validation, and consistent support they lacked. This could involve com-

forting yourself when distressed, setting healthy boundaries (for yourself and others), and celebrating your successes. This builds new, positive internal experiences.

- **Trauma-Informed Therapy:** If past trauma is significant, working with a therapist who specializes in trauma and neurodivergence (e.g., EMDR, somatic experiencing) is essential. They can help process these old wounds safely and effectively.
- **Connection to DDD Mastery:** Recognizing and healing your "emotional children" is about addressing the root causes of chronic emotional patterns. It helps to disentangle current reactions from past wounds, reducing the intensity of ARA and the sting of RSD. By reparenting yourself with compassion and understanding, you foster an internal environment where genuine emotional security can thrive, allowing your entire emotional symphony to play in greater harmony.

*Section 7: Becoming the Emotional Adult: Integration and Empowerment*

The final step is about developing and embodying the qualities of an emotional adult – a version of yourself that can navigate the complexities of your emotional neurodivergence with wisdom, autonomy, and resilience. This involves cultivating self-differentiation and emotional intelligence, which for the DDD individual means consciously building skills that compensate for executive function challenges and leverage unique strengths.

- **The Challenge for DDD:** While the desire for autonomy and self-mastery is strong, the very traits of DDD (e.g., VTO, IMA, PUR) can make consistent self-regulation and independent decision-making feel like an uphill battle. It's easy to revert to old patterns, especially under stress, making the journey to "emotional adulthood" feel daunting.
- **Actionable Strategies for DDD:**
- **Self-Differentiation (Setting Boundaries with Purpose):** This involves maintaining a strong sense of self while remaining connected to others, without becoming enmeshed in their emotions or expectations. For DDD, this often means:
- **Clear Boundaries:** Practice saying "no" to requests that overwhelm your executive capacity (VTO) or deplete your emotional resources. Use "I-statements" to communicate your needs clearly and respectfully.
- **Autonomy in Decision-Making (DFR-Aligned Choices):** Make conscious choices about how you spend your time and energy, aligning them with your values and interests (tapping into DFR for intrinsic motivation). This is about deliberate action, not impulsive reactions.
- **Managing External Opinions:** Develop a stronger internal compass. Seek feedback from trusted sources, but learn to filter out unhelpful criticism, especially that which triggers RSD.
- **Emotional Intelligence (Conscious Skill-Building):** While DDD can present challenges in emotional processing, emotional intelligence can be intentionally cultivated.
- **Self-Awareness:** Continue practices from Section 1

(journaling, tracking) to deepen understanding of your own emotional patterns.

- **Self-Regulation:** Systematically apply strategies from Section 4 to manage emotional responses in real-time. Make this a deliberate practice (DRC).
- **Social Awareness:** Pay attention to non-verbal cues in others. If struggling with this (IMA), consider explicitly asking for clarification ("When you said X, what did you mean?").
- **Relationship Management:** Practice effective communication (Section 3) and conflict resolution skills. Focus on building relationships with people who understand and validate your neurodivergence.
- **Structured Reflection and Learning (TAMD, VTO):** Regularly review past emotional situations: What happened? How did I feel? What did I do? What worked? What didn't? What will I do differently next time? Use a template or checklist to make this a consistent "routine" (DRC) that overcomes VTO. This builds a feedback loop for continuous improvement, strengthening your **Delayed Access to Dynamic Memory (TAMD)** for emotional learning.
- **Connection to DDD Mastery:** Becoming an emotional adult is an ongoing process of integration. It's about accepting your neurodivergent emotional blueprint, leveraging your strengths, building compensatory strategies for challenges, and continuously learning from your experiences. By embracing self-differentiation and consciously developing emotional intelligence, you become the skilled conductor of your emotional symphony, capable of creating harmony and navigating discord with increasing

grace and power. You move from being swept away by the current to actively steering your emotional vessel with confidence and purpose.

## Conclusion: The Resonant Power of Your Symphony

Emotional neurodivergence is not a deficit to be overcome, but a unique facet of identity to be understood and integrated. For parents with DDD, whose emotional experiences are often amplified and intricately woven with their neurological wiring, the journey to emotional mastery is both challenging and profoundly rewarding. We have explored seven vital steps: recognizing, validating, expressing, regulating, transforming, healing past wounds, and stepping into the role of the emotional adult. Each step, carefully tailored to the nuances of the DDD brain, offers practical strategies for navigating the intricate symphony of your feelings.

Remember, you are not alone in this vibrant, complex emotional landscape. Your emotional intensity is a source of profound empathy and creativity, your sensitivity a window into deeper understanding. This journey is about learning to wield these powerful traits with intention, to conduct your inner orchestra with skill, and to create a life where your emotional neurodivergence is not a burden, but a resonant source of strength and authenticity. We are in this together, and together, we can redefine what it means to truly thrive emotionally.

7

# Navigating the Neurotypical Emotional Landscape: DDD Mastery in a World Unaccustomed to Deep Feeling

**Introduction: The Unspoken Disconnect**

For those with **Dopamine Deficit Disorder (DDD)**, the world often feels like a place calibrated for a different emotional frequency. We exist within a vibrant, rich inner landscape, where emotions can surge with an intensity that bewilders and sometimes overwhelms. This is the essence of **emotional neurodivergence** – a way of experiencing feelings that deviates significantly from the neurotypical norm. Our emotions are not merely present; they are often a profound, deeply felt symphony, amplified by traits like

**Affective Reactivity Amplification (ARA)** and underpinned by a **Dopaminergic Reward Circuit (DRC)** that seeks novel and intense experiences.

Yet, this depth of feeling often clashes with a neurotypical world that, from our perspective, can seem emotionally "numbed" or at least significantly muted. We possess natural, robust, and often wonderfully healthy emotions, along with superpowered intuition and empathy. However, the ways we naturally express these feelings are frequently misunderstood or even pathologized by a society that values emotional conformity and subtle cues. This disconnect creates a dual challenge: not only must we learn to **regulate our own intense emotions**, but we must also **navigate a social landscape** where our authentic emotional expressions may be met with confusion, invalidation, or even subtle manipulation. The pressure to "tone down" our emotions to "blend in" or "fit the social norms" is immense, leading to exhausting emotional masking and internalized shame, deeply tied to **Rejection Sensitive Dysphoria (RSD)**.

This chapter will delve into both facets of this challenge. First, we will explore practical, neuro-affirmative strategies for self-regulation that resonate with the DDD brain's unique needs. Second, we will equip you with the tools to decode common neurotypical phrases that can be emotionally invalidating, offering methods to protect your emotional sovereignty and cultivate relationships that honor your authentic self. The goal is not to eradicate your emotional neurodivergence, but to master it, turning perceived weaknesses into powerful assets in a world still learning to appreciate the full spectrum of human feeling.

## *Section 1: Emotional Self-Regulation: Harmonizing Your Inner Symphony*

The journey of emotional self-regulation for individuals with DDD is unique. We often struggle with what is broadly termed "emotional regulation" – the ability to manage our intense emotional responses effectively. This isn't a deficit of feeling; rather, it's a challenge in modulating the powerful currents of emotions that flow through us. Our **Affective Reactivity Amplification (ARA)** means emotions can arise quickly and with overwhelming force, while our **Phenotype of Urgency for Reward (PUR)** can drive us towards immediate emotional relief, sometimes leading to impulsive or less-than-optimal coping mechanisms. This profound emotional intensity can profoundly impact our mood, relationships, and self-esteem.

While mainstream coping strategies exist, they often overlook the nuanced neurological underpinnings of DDD. We are not just looking to "copy and paste" generic advice. Instead, we acknowledge that our natural emotions are valid and vital, but the challenge lies in expressing them in ways that are understood and accepted by a neurotypical world. This often necessitates a conscious adjustment of our heightened sensitivity and empathy to fit social norms – a process of "toning down our emotions to blend in." This masking, while sometimes necessary for social navigation, comes at a significant emotional cost, contributing to burnout and feelings of inauthenticity.

However, our neurodivergent brains also come equipped with unique strengths. Our "superpowered intuition skills" often stem from a heightened observational capacity, a deeper empathetic resonance, and an ability to perceive patterns and subtle cues that others miss (related to aspects of our **Inattention Modulation Instability (IMA)** where attention can hyper-focus on specific details, or our **Delayed Access to Dynamic Memory (TAMD)** which allows for the rapid processing of vast amounts of sensory input). These skills can be invaluable for both controlling our own emotional reactions and rationally decoding the signals of others.

Here's how to lean into your strengths and cultivate effective self-regulation:

## 1. Intentional Emotional Reorientation: Shifting Your Focus with Purpose

For the DDD brain, simply telling oneself to "think positive" is often insufficient. Our **Drive for Novelty and Risk (DFR)** and the **Dopaminergic Reward Circuit (DRC)** respond best to active engagement and novel stimuli. We need strategies that actively re-engage our attention and dopamine pathways away from intense negative loops.

- **Beyond "Think Happy Thoughts":** When anger or sadness overwhelms, directly confronting the emotion can be counterproductive. Instead, aim to *redirect* your internal focus towards something genuinely engaging and positive.
- **Engaging Distractions (DFR-aligned):** This isn't avoidance, but a strategic pause. If you feel angry, immerse yourself in a creative project, a challenging puzzle, or a new piece of music that captivates your attention. The novelty and problem-solving elements can provide a dopamine

hit that shifts your internal state. If you feel sad, actively seek out content (a funny video, a compelling short story) that provides a distinct emotional shift.

- **Structured Gratitude:** Rather than a general gratitude list, focus on *specific, sensory details* of things that make you grateful. "I am grateful for the warmth of the sun on my skin" is more engaging than "I am grateful for the weather." This level of detail engages attention (counteracting IMA) and activates reward pathways.
- **Sensory Reset:** Engage your senses in a calming or uplifting way. Light a favorite candle, listen to a soothing playlist (curated for your specific preferences, appealing to DRC), or engage in mindful eating of a preferred texture.
- **Why it works for DDD:** This approach leverages the brain's natural desire for novelty and reward, making the shift from negative to positive more intrinsically motivating and less of an uphill battle against **Inattention Modulation Instability (IMA).** It's about providing an alternative, more rewarding pathway for your attention and dopamine.

## 2. Strategic Control: Mastering Your Spheres of Influence

Given the challenges of **Volition and Task Organization (VTO)** and **Phenotype of Urgency for Reward (PUR),** controlling what we can in any situation is paramount. This involves proactive planning and conscious boundary setting to prevent emotional overwhelm and impulsive reactions.

- **Environmental Control (VTO & PUR Mitigation):** If

a situation or environment is stressful, actively seek to change it or escape it. This requires planning and decisive action, which can be challenging for VTO.

- **Pre-emptive Planning:** Before entering a potentially stressful environment, plan an "exit strategy" or a designated quiet space. Use timers or reminders to prompt breaks.
- **Proactive Problem-Solving:** If a recurring problem triggers intense emotions, activate your problem-solving skills (even if VTO makes it hard to start). Break down the problem into the smallest possible steps. "What is one tiny thing I can do right now?" Ask for help, utilizing your intuition to identify supportive individuals.
- **Boundary Setting (Protecting Your Energy):** When dealing with difficult people, avoiding them might not always be possible. Setting clear, firm boundaries is crucial.
- **Scripted Responses:** For known triggers, have pre-scripted phrases ready (e.g., "I'm not comfortable discussing that," "I need to step away from this conversation"). This bypasses PUR's impulsivity.
- **Controlled Engagement:** Recognize when to disengage. If a conversation becomes emotionally dysregulating, politely excuse yourself. This is an act of self-preservation, not avoidance of responsibility.
- **Why it works for DDD:** This strategy directly addresses the challenges of VTO by emphasizing proactive planning and small, actionable steps. It empowers you to exert agency in your environment, reducing the likelihood of being caught off guard and succumbing to impulsive, dysregulated responses (PUR).

### 3. Nourishing Your Emotional Ecosystem: Prioritizing Joy and Connection

Emotional well-being for DDD individuals is deeply intertwined with consistent engagement in activities that provide genuine satisfaction and connection. Our **Dopaminergic Reward Circuit (DRC)** thrives on these experiences, and consistently activating it can build resilience against negative emotional states.

- **Scheduled Passion Time (Leveraging DRC & DFR):** Make your hobbies and passions non-negotiable. Schedule dedicated time for them daily, even if it's just 15-20 minutes. This consistent dopamine release helps stabilize mood and provides a vital counterpoint to stress. For those with **Drive for Novelty and Risk (DFR)**, rotating through different passions or finding novel aspects within a hobby can keep engagement high.
- **Intentional Social Connection:** For those with DDD, who may experience RSD and the exhaustion of masking, choosing supportive relationships is crucial. Prioritize regular contact with friends or family members who understand and validate your neurodivergence.
- **"Dopamine Buddy" Systems:** Partner with someone who shares your interests or understands your challenges. Regular check-ins or shared activities can provide consistent, low-demand social connection.
- **Neurodivergent-Affirming Spaces:** Actively seek out communities (online or in-person) where you feel understood and accepted. This reduces the cognitive load of masking and provides a safe space for authentic emotional

expression.

- **Mindful Appreciation:** Cultivate a practice of appreciating the small joys in your life – a pet, a plant, a favorite piece of art. Engaging with these sources of joy mindfully can ground you and provide consistent, gentle dopamine boosts.

- **Why it works for DDD:** This strategy directly feeds the **Dopaminergic Reward Circuit (DRC)**, fostering positive emotional states and building resilience. By consciously prioritizing activities and relationships that genuinely resonate with your brain's reward system, you create a robust buffer against emotional challenges and reduce the likelihood of slipping into prolonged negative states.


**4. Proactive Shielding: Avoiding Emotional Triggers with Awareness**

While complete avoidance is impractical, intelligently minimizing exposure to known triggers is a powerful self-regulation strategy for DDD individuals, particularly given the rapid onset of **Affective Reactivity Amplification (ARA)** and the deep sting of **Rejection Sensitive Dysphoria (RSD)**.

- **Identifying Triggers (TAMD & IMA):** Use your emotional journal (from Section 1) to meticulously track specific topics, people, places, or media that consistently trigger intense negative emotions. Recognize the patterns, which can be challenging due to **Delayed Access to Dynamic Memory (TAMD)**, requiring conscious effort.

- **Steering Clear/Changing Subject (PUR Management):** If you know certain topics or people trigger intense emotions, consciously steer conversations away or politely change the subject. For those prone to impulsivity (PUR), this requires pre-meditation and practice.
- **Environmental Preparedness (VTO & IMA):** If avoiding certain places or events is impossible, plan ahead for coping mechanisms. This involves activating **Volition and Task Organization (VTO):**
- Identify a quiet corner or escape route.
- Bring sensory tools (headphones, fidget toy).
- Set a time limit for your stay.
- Have a "check-out" buddy.
- **Curated Media Consumption:** Be highly selective about the media and news sources you consume. Limit exposure to content that consistently makes you angry or sad, especially if it leads to rumination (challenging for IMA). Seek out alternative sources that provide balanced information without excessive emotional activation.
- **Why it works for DDD:** This strategy is about respecting your neurological wiring. By proactively identifying and mitigating triggers, you prevent the rapid escalation of ARA and protect yourself from the deep emotional wounds of RSD. It's not about being fragile, but about intelligent self-preservation and conserving precious emotional energy.

*Section 2: Decoding the Neurotypical Code: Protecting Your Emotional Sovereignty*

Living in a neurotypical-dominated world often means navigating communication styles that can be subtly, or overtly, invalidating to the neurodivergent experience. For individuals with DDD, whose emotional responses are often amplified (ARA) and who may be exquisitely sensitive to rejection (RSD), certain common phrases uttered by those with lower emotional intelligence can be particularly damaging. Our "superpowered intuition" can detect the incongruity and dismissal inherent in these phrases, but understanding *why* they hurt and *how* to respond effectively is crucial for protecting your emotional sovereignty. This section is not about "overcoming manipulation" in a combative sense, but about cultivating self-awareness, setting healthy boundaries, and choosing relationships that truly honor your depth.

**Beware of These Phrases and Reevaluate Your Relationships:**

**1. "I don't care."**

- **The Neurotypical Low EQ Perspective:** This phrase is used to deflect, dismiss, or indicate a complete lack of interest in another's feelings or experience. It's a blunt instrument of emotional unavailability.
- **The Impact on DDD:** For someone with **Affective Reactivity Amplification (ARA)**, who often feels deeply and struggles to contain intense emotions, this phrase is a

direct invalidation of their entire emotional world. It can trigger profound **Rejection Sensitive Dysphoria (RSD)**, making you question your worthiness of empathy and connection. It suggests your vulnerability is irrelevant, leading to isolation and emotional withdrawal.

- **DDD Mastery Response:** Recognize this phrase as a red flag of emotional immaturity, not a reflection of your value. Internally validate your feelings: "My feelings are valid, even if this person cannot acknowledge them." If safe, state your boundary: "I understand you may not care, but I am sharing this because it's important to me. If you're unable to listen, I will share with someone who can." Reevaluate the depth and safety of this relationship.

## 2. "You're too sensitive."

- **The Neurotypical Low EQ Perspective:** This is a classic gaslighting phrase used to dismiss another's valid emotional response and shift blame onto them. It trivializes feelings it doesn't understand.
- **The Impact on DDD:** This phrase is the ultimate trigger for **Rejection Sensitive Dysphoria (RSD)**. It weaponizes your inherent trait of deep feeling (ARA) as a flaw. It forces you to internalize shame for your neurodivergent emotional processing, leading to masking and a profound sense of isolation. It implies your emotional "volume" is wrong, rather than their "hearing" being limited.
- **DDD Mastery Response:** Reclaim your sensitivity as a superpower. "I am sensitive, and that allows me to experience the world deeply and empathize with others. Perhaps my sensitivity highlights something you are

choosing not to feel or acknowledge." Or simply, "My feelings are my own, and they are valid." Do not engage in arguments about your sensitivity. Your sensitivity is a strength, allowing you to perceive nuances, connect deeply, and experience life fully.

**3. "That's not my problem."**

- **The Neurotypical Low EQ Perspective:** A phrase used to evade responsibility, show a lack of accountability, and prioritize self-interest above all else, even when one's actions contribute to the issue.
- **The Impact on DDD:** DDD individuals often possess a strong sense of justice and interconnectedness, coupled with a drive to solve problems (even if VTO makes initiation hard). This dismissive phrase can be jarring and deeply frustrating. It can trigger feelings of helplessness or a desire to "fix" the other person's lack of accountability, which can be draining.
- **DDD Mastery Response:** Recognize that you cannot force someone to care or take responsibility. Focus on your sphere of control. "I understand you see it that way. I will address this on my end." This is a moment to assess whether this person is truly a supportive ally or someone you need to protect your energy from. Your problem-solving drive (despite VTO challenges) is a gift, but it shouldn't be wasted on those unwilling to engage.

**4. "I know it all." / "You're wrong." / "I'm always right."**

- **The Neurotypical Low EQ Perspective:** These phrases

display arrogance, intellectual inflexibility, and a closed-mindedness that stifles learning and collaboration. They are about dominance, not understanding.

- **The Impact on DDD:** The **Drive for Novelty and Risk (DFR)** in DDD individuals often translates to an open-minded curiosity and a love for learning new perspectives. Confrontation with such rigid, dismissive attitudes can be frustrating and intellectually stifling.  It can feel like a direct assault on your desire for exploration and new insights, and can trigger **Rejection Sensitive Dysphoria (RSD)** if your differing opinion is met with contempt.
- **DDD Mastery Response:** Do not engage in a battle of wills. "I hear your perspective." "I appreciate you sharing that, and I have a different view." Focus on objective data or simply disengage. "It seems we have differing opinions on this, and that's okay." Your curiosity and adaptability are strengths; protect them from intellectual bullies.

### 5. "It's all your fault."

- **The Neurotypical Low EQ Perspective:** This is a pro-jection of blame, a refusal to take personal responsibility for mistakes or failures, seeking to scapegoat others.
- **The Impact on DDD:** Due to years of perceived failures stemming from unmanaged DDD traits and the pervasive sting of **Rejection Sensitive Dysphoria (RSD)**, DDD individuals are often highly susceptible to internalized blame. This phrase can reinforce deep-seated insecurities and exacerbate feelings of worthlessness, even if the blame is completely unjustified.
- **DDD Mastery Response:** Practice radical self-compassion.

"I take responsibility for my part, and I will not accept blame for yours." Objectively analyze the situation to discern genuine responsibility versus scapegoating. Your strong sense of justice should extend to yourself. Refuse to carry others' burdens of fault.

## 6. "It's not fair."

- **The Neurotypical Low EQ Perspective:** This phrase, when used by a low EQ individual, often indicates a victim mentality, a refusal to accept reality, or an expectation of entitlement.
- **The Impact on DDD:** DDD individuals often possess a heightened sense of justice and can be intensely frustrated by perceived unfairness in the world. However, when used by others to complain or whine, this phrase can become an emotional drain, leading to frustration, particularly for a brain that wants to solve problems (VTO) and move forward (DFR).
- **DDD Mastery Response:** While your own sense of fairness is valid, distinguish between authentic grievance and unproductive complaint. "Life isn't always fair, but we can control how we respond." Focus on realistic solutions or acceptance. Redirect the conversation to action or disengage.

## 7. "I can't."

- **The Neurotypical Low EQ Perspective:** This phrase, from a low EQ individual, often reflects a self-limiting belief, a lack of confidence, or an unwillingness to try or take risks.

- **The Impact on DDD:** For DDD individuals who often battle their own internal "I can't" narratives due to executive function challenges (**Volition and Task Organization (VTO), Inattention Modulation Instability (IMA)**), hearing this from others can be deeply disheartening or even triggering. It can reinforce their own struggles with initiation and perseverance.
- **DDD Mastery Response:** While respecting others' limitations, choose to surround yourself with empowering relationships. "What's one small step you *can* take?" Encourage (if appropriate), but do not allow their limitations to define your own potential. Reinforce your own belief in your abilities, even when faced with significant challenges.

## 8. "You make me feel..."

- **The Neurotypical Low EQ Perspective:** This is a classic phrase of emotional dumping, where an individual avoids taking ownership of their own emotions by blaming another for them.
- **The Impact on DDD:** For highly empathetic DDD individuals whose emotions can be amplified (**ARA**), absorbing the projected feelings of others can be incredibly draining and confusing. It can lead to guilt, confusion, and a compulsion to "fix" or take responsibility for another's emotional state, further exacerbating the challenges of **Rejection Sensitive Dysphoria (RSD)**.
- **DDD Mastery Response:** Recognize that you are not responsible for another's feelings. "I am responsible for my actions, and you are responsible for your feelings." Set

a clear boundary: "I cannot 'make' you feel anything. You choose how you react. We can discuss my actions, but not if you're blaming me for your emotions." This protects your emotional boundaries.

## 9. "Get over it." / "Get it together."

- **The Neurotypical Low EQ Perspective:** These are dismissive, invalidating phrases used to shut down another's emotions or struggles, often from a place of discomfort with intense feelings or a lack of empathy.
- **The Impact on DDD:** These phrases are devastatingly invalidating for individuals experiencing **Affective Reactivity Amplification (ARA)** and **Rejection Sensitive Dysphoria (RSD)**. They imply that your emotional experience is abnormal or a choice, reinforcing deepseated shame and forcing you to suppress genuine feelings, leading to further internal distress.
- **DDD Mastery Response:** These phrases are clear indicators of someone's inability to empathize or understand. Do not attempt to explain or justify yourself. Internally validate: "My feelings are valid, and I am processing this at my own pace." If necessary, "That comment is unhelpful and invalidating. I will talk to you when I'm ready." Protect your vulnerability from those who cannot meet you with compassion.

## Conclusion: Orchestrating Your Emotional Power

Navigating the emotional landscape of a neurotypical world while embracing your **Dopamine Deficit Disorder (DDD)** is a profound act of self-mastery. It requires a dual approach:

a deep dive into **emotional self-regulation** that is tailored to your unique neurological wiring, and a discerning understanding of how to **decode and respond to communication patterns** that might otherwise invalidate your experiences.

Your intense emotions, your profound empathy, and your unique intuitive insights are not burdens; they are powerful instruments in your emotional symphony. By mastering strategies for managing **Affective Reactivity Amplification (ARA)**, protecting yourself from **Rejection Sensitive Dysphoria (RSD)**, leveraging your **Drive for Novelty and Risk (DFR)** for positive engagement, and building scaffolding for your **Volition and Task Organization (VTO)** and **Inattention Modulation Instability (IMA)**, you move from passively experiencing your feelings to actively conducting them.

Embrace your full emotional spectrum. Recognize that the world may not always understand your profound depth, but that doesn't diminish its validity. By setting firm boundaries, seeking out neuro-affirming connections, and continuously practicing self-compassion, you protect your emotional sovereignty. You are not alone in this journey. Your emotional neurodivergence is a source of unique power, a wellspring of insight, and a testament to the beautiful complexity of the human spirit. Continue to explore, to learn, and to thrive, orchestrating a life that truly resonates with your authentic self.

8

# Unseen Repercussions: Understanding and Adapting Unintentional DDD Behaviors for Social Harmony

**I**ntroduction: The Subtle Social Minefield

For individuals navigating the world with **Dopamine Deficit Disorder (DDD)**, social interactions can often feel like traversing a complex, unseen minefield. Our unique neurological wiring, characterized by traits such as **Affective Reactivity Amplification (ARA), Phenotype of Urgency for Reward (PUR), Inattention Modulation Instability (IMA),** and challenges with **Volition and Task Organization (VTO),** means our behaviors naturally deviate from neurotypical expectations. Consequently, we may inadvertently make "mistakes" that, while completely unintentional, are often perceived by others as rude, careless, selfish, or even disrespectful. These seemingly minor missteps can accumulate, leading to unspoken judgments, social misunderstandings, and, ultimately, patterns of social rejection from those who lack an understanding or empathy for the DDD experience.

This chapter is dedicated to illuminating these common, yet often overlooked, social challenges. We will delve into specific instances where DDD-related behaviors can inadvertently create friction in social situations, exploring the underlying neurobiological reasons *why* these behaviors occur. More importantly, we will provide concrete, DDD-informed strategies for either avoiding these unintentional blunders or, when they occur, navigating their aftermath with grace and self-compassion. The ultimate goal is not to "fix" your neurodivergence, but to empower you to understand your social impact, leverage your inherent strengths, and cultivate deeper, more authentic social connections in a world that is still learning to appreciate the full spectrum of neurodiversity.

## *The Neurodivergent Social Landscape: Understanding the Mismatch*

The social world is largely built upon unwritten rules, subtle cues, and expectations of consistent executive function – areas where the DDD brain operates differently. Neurotypical social interactions often assume a baseline of sustained attention, seamless working memory, intuitive time management, and fluid conversational turn-taking. For someone with DDD, these assumptions create a constant cognitive load. Our attention may flit due to **IMA**, our memory for social nuances can be fleeting due to **Delayed Access to Dynamic Memory (TAMD)**, our urgency to speak (PUR) can override polite turn-taking, and our planning capabilities (VTO) might struggle with the spontaneity of social demands. This fundamental mismatch often leads to behaviors that are misinterpreted, not because of malicious intent, but because of differing operating systems. Understanding this inherent clash is the first step toward self-compassion and effective social adaptation.

*Common Unintentional DDD Social Blunders and Their DDD Roots*

Here, we explore specific scenarios where your DDD traits might inadvertently lead to social friction, alongside actionable strategies for navigating them.

## 1. The "Server Shuffle": Inattention and Working Memory Overload

**The Scenario:** You're at a bustling restaurant, perhaps a bit overwhelmed by the sensory input. You ask one server for a menu, another for your drink order, and a third for a refill, genuinely unaware that you're interacting with different individuals each time. You might even repeat your order or request across these different people.

**The DDD Roots:** This is a classic manifestation of **Inattention Modulation Instability (IMA)**. Your attention is fragmented, making it difficult to maintain focus on the identity of the specific person serving you. Working memory can also be strained, making it hard to retain the visual and contextual information (face, uniform, previous interaction) to distinguish between staff members. The rapid shifts in environment or task can easily pull your attention away, preventing the establishment of a consistent "social anchor." Your **Delayed Access to Dynamic Memory (TAMD)** might also hinder the quick recall of the last person who assisted you.

**The Unseen Repercussion:** To the neurotypical staff, this behavior can be perceived as inattentiveness, disrespect, or even a deliberate attempt to confuse or annoy them. They may feel ignored, frustrated by having to repeat information, or burdened by having to piece together your order from disparate requests. This can lead to silent judgment, reduced service quality, or a negative impression.

**DDD Mastery Strategies:**

- **"Visual Anchor" Focus:** Upon interaction, consciously make eye contact and try to notice one distinguishing feature (e.g., "blue scarf," "curly hair"). Use this as a mental tag for *your* server.
- **Verbal Confirmation:** If unsure, politely ask, "Are you my server?" or "Could you help me with my order, or should I wait for my server?" This proactively clarifies and shows respect.
- **Pre-emptive Apology/Explanation:** If you realize you've engaged multiple staff members, a quick, "My apologies, I just realized I've spoken to a few different people. Are you my main server?" can diffuse potential frustration.
- **External Reminders:** If with friends or family, discreetly

ask a trusted companion to help you track your server.

## 2. The "Loud Hyperfocus" Echo Chamber: Impulsivity and Auditory Filtering

**The Scenario:** You're engrossed in a phone conversation, deeply fascinated or excited by the topic. Unbeknownst to you, your voice gradually rises, until you're virtually shouting, disrupting the peace of those around you in a public space.

**The DDD Roots:** This is a powerful demonstration of **ADHD Hyperfocus**, often driven by the **Drive for Novelty and Risk (DFR)** when engaged in a stimulating conversation. When hyperfocus takes over, the brain's filtering mechanisms (part of IMA's difficulty with selective attention) can dim sensory input from the external environment, including your own vocal volume. Coupled with **Phenotype of Urgency for Reward (PUR)**, the compelling need to communicate your thoughts or hear the other person can override self-monitoring for appropriate volume. Impulsivity means the volume increases before conscious recognition.

**The Unseen Repercussion:** Others perceive this as rude, inconsiderate, or a blatant disregard for their privacy and peace. They may assume you are intentionally being disruptive, self-absorbed, or attempting to draw attention to yourself. This can lead to annoyance, embarrassment for your companions, and damage to your social reputation.

**DDD Mastery Strategies:**

- **"Volume Check" Reminders:** Set a mental trigger: every time you pause in conversation, do a quick self-check on your volume. Use an app that gives haptic feedback for loud environments.

- **Headphones/Earphones as Default:** Make wearing headphones your go-to in public spaces. This improves audio clarity, reducing the need to raise your voice, and also serves as a visual cue to others that you are in a private conversation.
- **Pre-emptive Apology & Relocation:** If you must speak loudly (e.g., poor reception), briefly apologize at the outset ("Apologies for the volume, bad signal!") and move to a more private area if possible.
- **"Conversation Buffer" Space:** When starting a call in public, consciously seek out a quieter, less populated area away from others.


## 3. The "Ephemeral Order": Executive Function and Object Permanence in Shared Spaces

**The Scenario:** You finish a meal at a restaurant, or check out of a hotel room, leaving behind a chaotic mess of discarded napkins, wrappers, forgotten items, or general disorder. You genuinely don't notice the mess, or if you do, the executive function required to clean it up feels insurmountable in the moment.

**The DDD Roots:** This directly relates to **Executive Dysfunction**, particularly impacting **Volition and Task Organization (VTO)**. Planning, prioritizing, and initiating cleanup tasks are incredibly difficult. The "out of sight, out of mind" phenomenon, a facet of **Inattention Modulation Instability (IMA)**, means that once an item is no longer immediately relevant, it ceases to exist in your conscious attention. The perceived overwhelming nature of "cleaning up" can also trigger **Volition and Task Organization (VTO)** paralysis.

**The Unseen Repercussion:** Staff perceive this as extreme carelessness, disrespect, or even entitlement. They may feel taken advantage of, burdened with excessive cleanup, or be forced to charge additional fees for damages or deep cleaning. This can harm your reputation as a considerate guest or patron.

**DDD Mastery Strategies:**

- **"Pre-Exit" Alarms:** Set a phone alarm 15-30 minutes before you need to leave a restaurant or check out of a hotel room. Label the alarm clearly: "Restaurant Cleanup!" or "Hotel Room Scan!"
- **Visual Checklist/Mnemonic:** For hotel rooms, have a simple mental (or even physical) checklist: "Bed, Bath, Desk, Door." Quickly scan each area.
- **"Micro-Cleanup" Habits:** Instead of waiting for a big cleanup, practice clearing small items as you go. One napkin at a time, one wrapper into the bin. This reduces the overwhelming task into manageable micro-steps that are easier for VTO.
- **"Body Doubling" (if applicable):** If with a trusted companion, ask them to do a quick "final sweep" with you or offer verbal prompts.

## 4. The "Impulsive Interruption": The Urgency of Thought and Turn-Taking Troubles

**The Scenario:** In a group conversation, you frequently cut people off, finish their sentences, or jump in with your own thoughts before they've completed theirs. You're not trying to be rude; your brain is just processing rapidly, and the urgent thought feels like it *must* come out now before you lose it.

**The DDD Roots:** This is a hallmark of **Phenotype of Urgency for Reward (PUR)**. Your thoughts race, and there's an immediate, almost compulsive, drive to express them. The fear of forgetting a brilliant idea (due to challenges with working memory) can make waiting feel physically uncomfortable. **Inattention Modulation Instability (IMA)** can also make it difficult to accurately track conversational rhythm, subtle pauses, and non-verbal cues that signal another person is not yet finished.

**The Unseen Repercussion:** Others perceive this as disrespectful, impatient, or as if you are only interested in your own thoughts. It can make them feel unheard, unimportant, and lead to frustration or disengagement from conversation with you.

**DDD Mastery Strategies:**

- **"Hold That Thought" Technique:** When an urgent thought arises, briefly acknowledge it mentally: "Okay, got that thought. Now listen." Physically, you can tap your finger discreetly on your leg or clench your fist to ground yourself.
- **Active Listening Practice:** Consciously focus on repeating back what the other person said in your mind (or even quietly to yourself) before formulating your response. This slows down your internal processing.
- **Non-Verbal Cues:** Train yourself to look for physical cues that someone is about to finish (e.g., eye contact, a slight

lean back).

- **Apologize and Redirect:** If you interrupt, quickly apologize ("Oh, sorry, I cut you off!") and invite them to continue ("Please, what were you saying?").
- **"Parking Lot" for Ideas:** In meetings, have a notepad to quickly jot down ideas you don't want to forget, so you can then fully listen without the pressure to interrupt.

## 5. The "Time Blindness" Ripple Effect: Executive Dysfunction in Temporal Awareness

**The Scenario:** You consistently arrive late for appointments, social gatherings, or deadlines, despite your best intentions. You genuinely misjudge how long tasks will take or how long it will take to get somewhere, often due to getting hyperfocused on a preceding task.

**The DDD Roots:** This is a core challenge of **Executive Dysfunction**, particularly impacting **Volition and Task Organization (VTO)** and **Inattention Modulation Instability (IMA)**. "Time blindness" is a common DDD phenomenon where the future is perceived as an abstract, infinite expanse, and the past quickly fades (TAMD). It's difficult to accurately estimate time, transition between tasks, or initiate the "getting ready" process. Hyperfocus can make you lose track of time entirely.

**The Unseen Repercussion:** Others perceive chronic lateness as disrespectful, unreliable, or a sign that you don't value their time. It can cause inconvenience, missed opportunities, and erode trust in both professional and personal relationships.

**DDD Mastery Strategies:**

- **"Time Doubling":** Assume every task will take twice as long as you initially estimate.
- **Pre-alarms & Transition Alarms:** Set multiple alarms. An alarm for "start getting ready," another for "leave the house," and a final one for "arrival buffer."
- **External Time Cues:** Use visible clocks, timers, or smart devices that give audible time announcements.
- **"Ready-to-Go" Bags:** For recurring events (e.g., going to the gym, work), pack essentials the night before.
- **Proactive Communication:** If you realize you're going to be late, communicate immediately and give an honest (but not overly detailed) estimate of your arrival. "I'm running a bit behind, I expect to be there in 10 minutes."

## 6. The "Information Avalanche": Passion, Hyper-focus, and Conversational Flow

**The Scenario:** When discussing a topic you're passionate about (a special interest, a new discovery, a recent project), you inadvertently launch into a monologue, overwhelming your listener with a torrent of detailed information without noticing their disengagement cues.

**The DDD Roots:** This is deeply rooted in the **Drive for Novelty and Risk (DFR)**, which fuels intense passion and hyperfocus on specific interests. When activated, the urge to share this knowledge is powerful (PUR). **Inattention Modulation Instability (IMA)** can make it difficult to read subtle social cues of disinterest (e.g., glazed eyes, shifting posture, looking away) or to filter irrelevant details. The sheer volume of information in your brain can feel urgent to download.

**The Unseen Repercussion:** Others can feel overwhelmed, bored, or trapped. They may perceive you as self-absorbed, lacking social awareness, or even condescending. This can lead to them avoiding conversations with you or disengaging mentally.

**DDD Mastery Strategies:**

- **"The Conversation Sandwich":** Start with a key point, then *ask a question* to gauge interest, then share more, then ask another question. This creates a back-and-forth flow.
- **"Topic Parking":** Before launching into a deep dive, briefly state your enthusiasm: "I'm really excited about X, but I don't want to overwhelm you. Are you up for a deep dive, or just the highlights?"
- **Self-Monitoring Prompts:** Discreetly set a timer for 2-3 minutes. When it buzzes, prompt yourself to ask a question or invite the other person's input.
- **Observe Engagement Cues:** Consciously practice noticing non-verbal cues. If they are looking away, fidgeting, or giving brief answers, it's a sign to pause and re-engage them.
- **Find Your Audience:** Seek out spaces and people who share your special interests and genuinely appreciate deep dives. Leverage online communities for passionate discussions where you won't overwhelm others.

*Leveraging Your DDD Strengths for Social Flourishing: A Proactive Approach*

While understanding and adapting to social challenges is crucial, true DDD mastery involves actively leveraging your inherent strengths.

### 1. Seek Professional Neurodivergent-Affirming Help:

- **Why for DDD:** A proper diagnosis (if not already obtained) provides a crucial framework for understanding your unique brain. Work with therapists, coaches, or specialists who are knowledgeable about DDD and neurodivergence. They can help you develop personalized strategies for executive function, emotional regulation (ARA), and social skills, without pathologizing your neurodivergence. This guidance can prevent internalized shame (RSD) and provide concrete tools for navigating your specific challenges.

### 2. Find Your Niche and Build on Strengths:

- **Why for DDD:** Aligning your life, especially your career and passions, with your DDD strengths is paramount for well-being and social confidence. Your **Drive for Novelty and Risk (DFR),** hyperfocus, creativity, resilience, and unique perspective can be immense assets. Seek environments where these traits are valued, rather than suppressed. For example, a career that allows for deep dives into stimulating projects (leveraging hyperfocus) might be more fulfilling than a role requiring constant, fragmented attention.

## 3. Manage Your Challenges with DDD-Specific Tools and Strategies:

- **Why for DDD:** Generic advice often fails because it doesn't account for the unique executive function deficits (**VTO, IMA, TAMD**). Embrace external scaffolding.
- **Gamification:** Turn daunting tasks into games (appealing to DRC) to boost motivation.
- **Body Doubling:** Work alongside someone (in person or virtually) to leverage external accountability and focus.
- **Visual Aids:** Use whiteboards, mind maps, and color-coded systems to externalize organizational tasks.
- **Time Management Tools:** Beyond simple alarms, explore apps that use visual timers or pomodoro techniques that align with how your brain perceives time.

## 4. Cultivate a Supportive Ecosystem:

- **Why for DDD:** Battling social misunderstandings alone amplifies **Rejection Sensitive Dysphoria (RSD)**. Surround yourself with people who understand, accept, and celebrate your neurodivergence.
- **Neuro-Affirming Community:** Actively seek out online forums, local meetups, or support groups for DDD or neurodivergent individuals. Shared experiences foster validation and reduce isolation.
- **Educate Loved Ones:** Share resources and explain your DDD traits to close friends and family, helping them understand your unintentional behaviors and fostering

empathy.

- **Mentorship/Coaching:** Connect with individuals who have successfully navigated similar challenges and can offer guidance and encouragement.

## 5. Celebrate Your Authentic Achievements:

- **Why for DDD:** The constant battle with executive function and social misunderstandings can chip away at self-esteem, making **Rejection Sensitive Dysphoria (RSD)** worse. Consciously celebrating your accomplishments, no matter how small, is vital for activating your **Dopaminergic Reward Circuit (DRC)** and reinforcing positive self-perception.
- **Non-Normative Successes:** Celebrate not just traditional successes, but also the unique ways you overcome challenges or leverage your neurodivergence. Did you manage to start that daunting task? Celebrate it! Did you successfully navigate a tricky social situation? Acknowledge your effort.
- **Self-Rewards:** Tie small, dopamine-boosting rewards to completed tasks or successful social engagements. This creates a positive feedback loop for your brain.

## Conclusion: Embracing Your Social Authenticity

Unintentional social blunders are an inherent part of the DDD experience when navigating a neurotypical world. They are not a reflection of your character or intent, but rather a byproduct of a beautifully unique neurological design. By understanding the underlying DDD traits that contribute to these moments, you gain the power to respond with self-compassion, implement effective strategies, and choose environments and relationships that truly nurture your well-being.

This chapter has provided a roadmap for understanding the "unseen repercussions" of your behaviors and for cultivating social harmony without sacrificing your authentic self. Your journey is one of continuous learning, adaptation, and self-advocacy. Embrace your distinct way of being; it is a source of immense creativity, empathy, and resilience. By mastering these social dynamics, you not only improve your reputation and relationships but also unlock the full potential of your emotional self, allowing your unique DDD light to shine brightly in any social landscape.

9

# Weaving Your Web: Authentic Networking and Finding Your Tribe as a DDD Neurodivergent Adult

**I**ntroduction: **The Authentic Connection Imperative**

In the intricate dance of modern life, networking is often presented as a non-negotiable path to success—a labyrinth of handshakes, small talk, and strategic connections. For many, this process feels intuitive, a natural extension of social engagement. However, for neurodivergent adults, particularly those navigating the unique landscape of **Dopamine Deficit Disorder (DDD)**, traditional networking paradigms can feel like an alien ritual, fraught with anxiety and misunderstanding. Our brains are wired differently, affecting sociability, attention, executive function, sensory processing, and emotional regulation. This can make the perceived demands of networking – seamless communication, fluid social mirroring, sustained attention to non-preferred tasks, and navigating sensory-rich environments – seem overwhelmingly daunting.

Neurodivergence, encompassing conditions like Autism Spectrum Disorder, ADHD (a close cousin to DDD), dyslexia, and others, represents a profound variation in human cognition. For DDD individuals, this means our **Inattention Modulation Instability (IMA)** can hinder sustained attention to conversational nuances, our **Volition and Task Organization (VTO)** challenges can impede follow-through, and our **Affective Reactivity Amplification (ARA)** can make social anxieties feel disproportionately intense. The fear of misunderstanding, misinterpretation, or triggering **Rejection Sensitive Dysphoria (RSD)** can create a formidable barrier to authentic connection.

Yet, networking does not have to be a source of dread. In fact, when approached through a neuro-affirmative lens, it can transform into a profoundly rewarding experience. This chapter will guide you through weaving your own authentic web of connections, leveraging your unique DDD strengths to find your "tribe" – those who truly see, understand, and value you. We will explore practical strategies for engaging in meaningful interactions, preparing effectively while respecting your neurological limits, and ultimately, embracing your authentic self to build a profound sense of belonging in a world that often demands conformity.

## The Neurodivergent Networking Imperative: Why We Seek Our Tribe

The traditional networking environment often operates on unstated assumptions that clash with the DDD experience. These settings frequently demand sustained, flexible attention (difficult with IMA), rapid social processing (challenging for TAMD), suppression of sensory sensitivities (overwhelming for ARA-prone individuals), and the performance of neurotypical social rituals like small talk, which can feel draining and inauthentic for those whose brains are wired for depth over superficiality (DFR). The immense cognitive and emotional labor involved in masking—suppressing natural stims, forcing eye contact, scripting responses—leads to profound emotional exhaustion and can exacerbate **Rejection Sensitive Dysphoria (RSD)** when the mask inevitably slips or is perceived negatively.

Despite these hurdles, the inherent human need for belonging remains powerful. For DDD individuals, who may have experienced chronic feelings of difference, isolation, or misunderstanding throughout their lives, finding genuine connection is not merely a social nicety; it is a fundamental imperative for well-being. Our deep empathy, capacity for hyperfocus on shared interests, and drive for meaningful engagement (**Drive for Novelty and Risk (DFR)**) make us uniquely suited for forming profound, authentic bonds—if we can bypass the superficial barriers of traditional networking. We seek not just connections, but resonance; not just opportunities, but a sense of being truly seen and valued.

*Section 1: Seeking Your People: Curating Your Authentic Network*

The cornerstone of successful networking for a DDD individual lies in shifting the focus from quantity to quality: finding people who truly align with your interests, values, and goals. These are the individuals who will intuitively understand, genuinely support, and deeply inspire you. This is where you find your people, your tribe.

For many DDD adults, a lifetime of feeling "too different" or "too much" often leads to a pattern of masking. The fear of rejection, intensified by **Rejection Sensitive Dysphoria (RSD)**, compels us to conform to neurotypical standards, suppressing our authentic selves. However, the true liberation in networking comes from recognizing that you don't need to change who you are to be accepted. Instead, the goal is to find environments and individuals who celebrate your neurodiversity as a gift.

Here are neuro-affirmative strategies for finding these meaningful connections:

## 1. Online Communities: Leveraging Controlled Engagement & Shared Hyperfocus

**Why it Works for DDD:** Online platforms are a sanctuary for many neurodivergent individuals because they offer unparalleled control over the pace, method, and sensory input of interactions. This directly addresses challenges related to **Inattention Modulation Instability (IMA)** by allowing for asynchronous communication (no immediate pressure to respond), reduced sensory overwhelm (no loud environments, bright lights, or unexpected touch), and the ability to engage from your personal comfort zone. Furthermore, the inherent structure of online groups, often centered around specific interests, naturally fosters environments conducive to **Hyperfocus** and the **Drive for Novelty and Risk (DFR)**, allowing for deep dives into shared passions without the demands of small talk.

**Practical Tips for Maximizing Online Engagement:**

- **Hyper-Niche Exploration:** Seek out highly specific online forums, Discord servers, Facebook groups, or subreddits related to your most intense interests, hobbies, or even niche DDD-specific topics. The more specific, the higher the chance of finding deeply resonant connections.
- **Passive Participation First:** Don't feel pressured to jump in immediately. Spend time observing the dynamics, learning the unspoken rules, and understanding the common topics. This low-pressure entry allows your brain to process without being overwhelmed.
- **Leverage Asynchronous Communication:** Use the ability to craft thoughtful responses over time. This bypasses the impulsivity of **Phenotype of Urgency for Reward (PUR)** and the verbal processing challenges (IMA) that can make real-time conversations difficult.
- **Manage Notifications:** Implement strategies to prevent **Inattention Modulation Instability (IMA)** from leading to distraction or overwhelm. Turn off non-essential notifications, or schedule specific times to check your communities.
- **Consider Voice Chat (Optional & Structured):** If com-

fortable, explore voice channels within communities. These can offer a more fluid interaction but ensure they are structured (e.g., specific discussion times) and allow for easy exit if sensory overwhelm (ARA) occurs.

## 2. Attending Aligned Events: Strategic Immersion & Sensory Management

**Why it Works for DDD:** While seemingly counter-intuitive, in-person events related to your passions can be highly effective because they inherently provide a shared interest, reducing the need for strained small talk and allowing for natural **Hyperfocus** on the event's content. The inherent purpose of the event provides a clear social script, and the excitement can tap into your **Dopaminergic Reward Circuit (DRC)**, making engagement more rewarding.

**Practical Tips for Successful Event Navigation:**

- **Pre-Event Research & Goal Setting (VTO & IMA):** Research the event schedule, speakers, and attendees beforehand. Set realistic, micro-goals (e.g., "Ask one question," "Talk to two new people about X topic"). This reduces **Volition and Task Organization (VTO)** paralysis and helps direct your attention (IMA).
- **Sensory Management Plan (ARA & IMA):** Anticipate sensory triggers. Bring noise-canceling headphones, wear comfortable clothing, identify quiet zones or "escape routes" within the venue. Plan for short breaks to regulate your **Affective Reactivity Amplification (ARA)**.
- **"Conversation Starters" (TAMD & VTO):** Prepare a

few open-ended questions related to the event's topic. This provides a mental scaffold, reducing anxiety about initiating conversation and aiding **Delayed Access to Dynamic Memory (TAMD)** in retrieval of relevant information.

- **Focused Engagement:** Instead of trying to meet everyone, focus on truly engaging with a few individuals who spark your interest. Ask follow-up questions about the event content to steer away from uncomfortable small talk.
- **Post-Event Follow-Up (VTO & TAMD):** Exchange contact information. Set a reminder immediately to follow up within 24-48 hours. Have a template for initial outreach to make **Volition and Task Organization (VTO)** easier.

### 3. Reaching Out to Inspirations: Targeted Engagement & Leveraging DFR

**Why it Works for DDD:** DDD individuals often have a powerful **Drive for Novelty and Risk (DFR)** and a capacity for intense admiration for individuals who inspire them. This inherent interest provides significant intrinsic motivation, overcoming the **Volition and Task Organization (VTO)** challenges often associated with cold outreach. When you genuinely admire someone, your communication is authentic and compelling.

**Practical Tips for Meaningful Outreach:**

- **Personalized & Concise Messaging:** Avoid generic templates. Reference specific work, ideas, or achievements that resonated with you. Be brief, respecting their time (e.g., an email, LinkedIn message, or respectful comment on their content).

- **Focus on Genuine Curiosity:** Frame your outreach as a desire to learn or express appreciation, not solely to gain something. "I was so struck by your work on X; I'd love to know more about Y."
- **Respectful Follow-Up:** If you don't hear back, don't take it personally (RSD). They are likely busy. A single, polite follow-up after a week is generally acceptable.
- **Offer Value (If Possible):** If you have a unique skill or insight that could genuinely benefit them, offer it briefly. "I noticed X on your website, and my expertise in Y might offer a new perspective."

*Section 2: Being Ready: Proactive Strategies for Authentic Engagement*

Networking, by its very nature, can be unpredictable and spontaneous. For neurodivergent adults, whose brains often thrive on predictability and struggle with uncertainty due to challenges with **Volition and Task Organization (VTO)** and **Inattention Modulation Instability (IMA)**, this can amplify anxiety. However, "being ready" isn't about rigid scripting; it's about developing mental, emotional, and practical scaffolding that supports your authentic engagement and mitigates the impact of DDD challenges.

**1. Setting Realistic, DDD-Friendly Goals: Process Over**

**Perfection (VTO & DRC)**

**Why it Works for DDD:** Overwhelm is a significant barrier for DDD. Setting micro-goals that focus on the *process* of networking, rather than just the *outcome*, reduces **Volition and Task Organization (VTO)** paralysis and provides more frequent opportunities for the **Dopaminergic Reward Circuit (DRC)** to activate, reinforcing positive behavior.

**Practical Tips:**

- **Micro-Goals:** Instead of "get a job," try "attend one networking event," "talk to one new person for 5 minutes," or "send one follow-up email."
- **Energy Budgeting:** Before an event, estimate your "social battery" level. Decide how long you realistically can engage before needing a break or leaving.
- **Process-Oriented Metrics:** Define success by effort, not outcome. "I successfully initiated a conversation," rather than "I got a job lead."

## 2. Strategic Research: Equipping Your Brain (TAMD & IMA for Information Gathering)

**Why it Works for DDD:** Research pre-loads your brain with conversational "hooks" and reduces the pressure of real-time information retrieval (difficult for TAMD). It provides concrete topics for discussion, appealing to the DDD preference for depth over small talk (DFR), and helps direct attention (IMA).

**Practical Tips:**

- **Targeted Information:** For individuals, look up their recent projects or interests on LinkedIn. For events, review the agenda, speaker bios, or recent news related to the topic.
- **"Anchor Questions":** Prepare 2-3 open-ended questions related to your research that you can deploy if conversation stalls.
- **Curate Your "About Me" Facts:** Think of 2-3 interesting facts about yourself or your work that you can share when asked, avoiding rambling (PUR).

## 3. Crafting Your Authentic Pitch: Concise Communication & Confidence (PUR & IMA)

**Why it Works for DDD:** Having a prepared, concise self-introduction reduces cognitive load in the moment, minimizes the risk of rambling (due to **Phenotype of Urgency for Reward (PUR)**) or getting sidetracked (IMA), and allows your unique value to shine through.

**Practical Tips:**

- **The "DDD Superpower" Twist:** Beyond name and role, briefly weave in how your neurodivergence enhances your work. E.g., "I'm a designer, and my hyperfocus allows me to dive deep into complex visual systems and find creative solutions."
- **Multi-Modal Practice:** Practice your pitch aloud, record it, or rehearse with a trusted friend. This helps solidify it in your **Delayed Access to Dynamic Memory (TAMD)** and builds confidence.

- **Tailor for Context:** Have a slightly shorter version for quick introductions and a slightly longer one for more in-depth conversations.

## 4. Managing Social Energy & Overwhelm: Pacing for Sustainability (ARA & IMA)

**Why it Works for DDD:** Networking demands significant cognitive and emotional energy for DDD individuals, often leading to rapid fatigue or **Affective Reactivity Amplification (ARA)**. Proactive energy management is crucial for sustainability.

**Practical Tips:**

- **Pre-Event Decompression:** Arrive early to scout the venue and find a quiet spot, or engage in a calming activity beforehand.
- **Scheduled Breaks:** During an event, excuse yourself for regular, planned "recharge" breaks in a quiet area.
- **"Social Battery" Check-ins:** Regularly assess your energy level. When it dips, activate your exit strategy or move to a less demanding interaction.
- **Sensory Toolkit:** Carry discreet items like noise-canceling earplugs, a preferred fidget toy, or a calming scent to help regulate sensory input (IMA).

## 5. Follow-Up Strategies: Sustaining Connection (VTO & TAMD)

**Why it Works for DDD:** The excitement of an interaction can fade, and the subsequent task of following up can trigger **Volition and Task Organization (VTO)** paralysis or be forgotten due to **Delayed Access to Dynamic Memory (TAMD)**. Structured follow-up is essential.
**Practical Tips:**

- **Immediate Capture:** Right after meeting someone, make a quick note on their business card or in your phone about something specific you discussed. This aids TAMD.
- **24-Hour Rule:** Aim to send a personalized follow-up email or LinkedIn message within 24 hours while the memory is fresh.
- **Template with Personalization:** Have a basic template for follow-ups, but always customize it with specific details from your conversation. This makes VTO easier.
- **CRM/Reminder System:** Use a simple spreadsheet or a reminder app to track who you've met, when you followed up, and when a gentle "check-in" might be appropriate.

*Section 3: Being Yourself: Embracing Your DDD Identity in Networking*

The most pivotal aspect of networking as a DDD adult is authenticity. Networking is not about contorting yourself into a neurotypical mold; it's about expressing your true self and attracting others who resonate with who you genuinely are. For too long, many neurodivergent individuals have been conditioned to believe that their "too much-ness"—too impulsive (PUR), too distracted (IMA), too emotional (ARA), too sensitive (RSD)—is a flaw requiring constant suppression.

**The Cost of Masking for DDD:**

Masking—the conscious or unconscious suppression of neurodivergent traits to fit in—is an exhausting and ultimately unsustainable strategy. It leads to profound emotional burnout, increased anxiety, and a feeling of inauthenticity that prevents genuine connection. When you mask, you inadvertently invite connections based on a false premise, exacerbating **Rejection Sensitive Dysphoria (RSD)** when the mask becomes too heavy to maintain, and the fear of "being found out" looms. True belonging cannot exist where authenticity is absent.

**Highlighting Your DDD Strengths in Networking:**

Instead of apologizing for your neurodiversity, learn to frame it as a source of strength and creativity. These very traits, often misunderstood, are powerful assets in building meaningful relationships:

- **Hyperfocus & Deep Dive:** Your ability to intensely concentrate means you can engage in conversations with profound depth, offering unique insights and truly listening when a topic captures your attention. This allows for deep, meaningful connections.
- **Creativity & Out-of-the-Box Thinking:** Your divergent thinking patterns lead to innovative ideas and solutions, making you a valuable and fascinating conversationalist

who approaches problems from fresh angles.

- **Empathy & Intuition (ARA):** Your heightened emotional awareness, though sometimes overwhelming (**Affective Reactivity Amplification (ARA)**), can make you incredibly empathetic and intuitive, allowing you to connect with others on a deeper emotional level.
- **Passion & Enthusiasm (DFR):** When you're genuinely interested, your **Drive for Novelty and Risk (DFR)** fuels an infectious enthusiasm that can be highly engaging and inspiring to others.
- **Resilience:** Having navigated a world not built for your brain, you often possess immense resilience and a unique perspective on overcoming challenges, making you a source of quiet strength and inspiration.

**Strategic Disclosure: When and How to Share Your Neurodivergence:**

Deciding whether and when to disclose your DDD is a personal choice based on safety, trust, and context.

- **Context is Key:** In professional settings, you might focus on how your neurodivergence translates into strengths (e.g., "My ADHD brain allows me to make connections others miss"). In social settings, disclose when you feel a sense of psychological safety and a genuine desire for deeper understanding.
- **Frame as Strength or Difference, Not Deficit:** "My brain works a bit differently, which means I'm highly creative, but I sometimes need a quiet space to process."

- **Educate Gently:** If you choose to disclose, be prepared to offer brief, accessible explanations.
- **Observe Reciprocity:** True belonging often involves reciprocal vulnerability. When others show openness, it creates a safe space for you to be more authentic.

The power of being yourself lies in attracting your true tribe—individuals and communities who value you for *who you are*, not who you pretend to be. This leads to connections that are not only more sustainable but also profoundly more fulfilling, reducing the need to mask and fostering a genuine sense of belonging.

**Conclusion: The Resonance of Authentic Connection**

Networking as a DDD neurodivergent adult is not about conforming to outdated norms; it's about forging authentic connections that honor your unique brain. By understanding the subtle ways your DDD traits can influence social interactions, proactively managing challenges, and, most importantly, embracing your authentic self, you transform networking from a daunting task into a journey of discovery and belonging.

Your distinct way of perceiving, processing, and interacting with the world is a powerful asset. Leverage your **hyperfocus**, your **creativity**, your **empathy**, and your **passion**. Navigate the social labyrinth with intention and self-compassion, knowing that every step towards authenticity is a step closer to finding your true tribe. The most profound connections are not built on superficial pleasantries, but on the rich, resonant vibrations of genuine understanding and mutual acceptance. Weave your web with threads of authenticity, and watch as a truly supportive and belonging community gathers around you.

# 10

# Conclusion

**I**ntroduction: **The Journey from Disconnect to Discovery**
This book has been a profound journey, an odyssey into the intricate landscape of the neurodivergent experience, particularly as it manifests in what we have redefined as **Dopamine Deficit Disorder (DDD)**. We began by acknowledging a pervasive, often unspoken, truth: the feeling of being fundamentally different, of living in an "unseen dimension" where the world operates on a frequency we can't quite tune into. This sense of being an outsider, a misfit, is not a personal failing but a profound consequence of a neurobiological reality. We have moved beyond the limiting and often stigmatizing label of "ADHD" to embrace "DDD," a term that precisely grounds this condition in its neurochemical essence – a dysregulation of the dopaminergic system, an

**"invisible emergency"** that profoundly impacts every facet of an individual's life.

Our exploration has been comprehensive, dissecting the very fabric of this experience. We have delved into the clinical definitions, understood the prevalence and complex etiologies, and examined the diverse ways DDD symptoms manifest, from challenges in attention and organization to the nuances of emotional regulation and impulse control. Crucially, we have illuminated the pervasive and often devastating impact of **stigma and discrimination**, revealing how societal misunderstanding and judgment amplify the inherent difficulties of DDD, creating unnecessary barriers to well-being and success.

But this book is far from a lament. It is a manifesto of empowerment, a guide to transformation. We have meticulously explored how the very traits often perceived as weaknesses are, in fact, unique strengths, particularly within the dynamic and innovative world of entrepreneurship. We have provided a roadmap for navigating the complexities of DDD, offering concrete strategies for self-management, fostering authentic connections, and advocating for a world that truly embraces neurodiversity. This concluding chapter serves as a synthesis of our journey, a powerful reaffirmation of the DDD paradigm, and a fervent call to action for building a future where every neurotype can not only survive but truly thrive.

*The Paradigm Shift: Reclaiming the Narrative of Dopamine Deficit Disorder*

At the heart of this book lies a fundamental paradigm shift: the redefinition of ADHD as **Dopamine Deficit Disorder (DDD)**. This is more than a mere change in terminology; it is a conceptual revolution designed to provide clarity, reduce stigma, and guide more effective interventions. By focusing on the underlying neurochemical dysregulation – specifically, the atypical functioning of dopamine pathways in key brain regions – we move beyond a purely behavioral description to a deeper, more accurate understanding.

We introduced a new lexicon, a precise language to articulate the lived experience of DDD:

- **Affective Reactivity Amplification (ARA):** The heightened intensity and rapid shifts in emotional responses.
- **Delayed Access to Dynamic Memory (TAMD):** The difficulty in accessing and utilizing information in real-time, often perceived as forgetfulness or slow processing.
- **Drive for Novelty and Risk (DFR):** The inherent craving for new, stimulating experiences, often leading to a preference for high-stakes situations or a struggle with routine.
- **Inattention Modulation Instability (IMA):** The fluctuating nature of attention, ranging from profound distraction to intense hyperfocus.
- **Phenotype of Urgency for Reward (PUR):** The compelling drive for immediate gratification and a low tolerance for delayed rewards.

- **Volition and Task Organization (VTO):** The significant challenges in initiating, planning, organizing, and sustaining effort on tasks, particularly those lacking immediate interest.
- **Dopaminergic Reward Circuit (DRC):** The core neurobiological system at play, often functioning atypically in DDD, impacting motivation and pleasure.

This new language is not just for clinicians; it is for you. It provides a framework for self-understanding, a means to articulate your internal experience, and a tool to communicate your needs with greater precision. It transforms vague complaints into definable neurobiological phenomena, fostering self-compassion and empowering effective self-advocacy.

## *The Dual Nature: Strengths and Challenges of the DDD Brain*

Throughout this book, we have emphasized that DDD is not solely a collection of deficits. It is a neurobiological difference that bestows a unique constellation of strengths, often overlooked in a neurotypical-centric world.

**The Superpowers of the DDD Brain:**

- **Unleashed Creativity and Innovative Thinking:** The divergent thinking patterns, the ability to connect disparate ideas, and the inherent drive for novelty (DFR) make DDD individuals natural innovators, capable of generating groundbreaking solutions.

- **Boundless Curiosity and Relentless Exploration:** An insatiable drive to learn and explore new opportunities, markets, and ideas, fueling entrepreneurial spirit and adaptability.
- **The Power of Hyperfocus:** When genuinely engaged, the capacity for intense, sustained concentration (IMA) allows for unparalleled productivity and mastery in areas of passion.
- **Unyielding Resilience and Rapid Adaptability:** A lifetime of navigating a world not built for their operating system cultivates extraordinary tenacity, problem-solving prowess, and the ability to pivot quickly in the face of adversity.
- **Calculated Risk-Taking and Bold Decisiveness:** The comfort with uncertainty and the drive for immediate action (PUR) can translate into a willingness to seize opportunities and make bold decisions that others might shy away from.
- **Profound Empathy and Intuition (ARA):** A heightened emotional sensitivity, while challenging, also fosters deep empathy, allowing for profound connections and intuitive understanding of others.
- **High Energy and Urgency:** When channeled effectively, the inherent drive and energy can fuel intense periods of productivity and sustained effort.

The Inherent Challenges:

However, we have also been unflinchingly honest about the challenges. These are not moral failings but direct consequences of the DDD neurobiology:

- Difficulties with executive functions (planning, organizing, initiating, sustaining tasks – VTO).
- Challenges in emotional regulation (ARA), leading to intense, sometimes overwhelming, emotional responses.
- Vulnerability to distraction (IMA) and difficulty with consistent attention on mundane tasks.
- A predisposition to impulsivity (PUR), which can lead to hasty decisions or actions.
- Struggles with working memory and information retrieval (TAMD).

Understanding this dual nature – the extraordinary gifts alongside the inherent challenges – is the cornerstone of effective self-management and advocacy. It moves us beyond a narrative of brokenness to one of unique wiring.

## *The External Burden: Navigating a World Not Built for DDD*

Beyond the internal complexities, this book has exposed the profound external pressures and systemic biases that compound the DDD experience. These are not individual failures, but societal shortcomings that create immense friction and suffering.

1. The Weight of Stigma and Discrimination (Chapter 2):
2. The pervasive negative attitudes, stereotypes, and outright discrimination surrounding ADHD/DDD create an invisible burden. This stigma, whether internalized or

external, erodes self-esteem, limits opportunities, and acts as a significant barrier to seeking and receiving crucial diagnosis and treatment. We saw how even well-intentioned but uninformed public perceptions can perpetuate misunderstanding.

3. Unintentional Social Missteps and Rejection (Chapter 8):

4. Our unique neurobiology often leads to behaviors that, while completely unintentional, are misinterpreted by neurotypical individuals as rude, careless, or disrespectful. From the "server shuffle" to the "loud hyperfocus" of a phone conversation, or the "time blindness" that leads to chronic lateness, these subtle social mismatches cause friction, leading to secret judgments and painful social rejection. We explored how our IMA, PUR, VTO, and TAMD can contribute to these misunderstandings, creating a cycle of frustration and isolation.

5. The Counter-Fire of Neuroplasticity (Chapter 9):

6. One of the most insidious burdens is how our own brain's incredible capacity for adaptation – neuroplasticity – can turn against us. In a constant effort to cope with unmanaged DDD traits and a neurotypical world, we develop compensatory mechanisms (e.g., perfectionism, procrastination-panic, emotional suppression). The tragic irony is that, through repeated use, these coping strategies become "wired" into our brains, transforming into full-blown comorbidities like anxiety, depression, or even addiction. Our brain, in its attempt to survive, inadvertently creates new patterns of suffering.

7. The Incentive Trap (Chapter 10):

8. Our societal systems – educational, professional, financial, and even medical – are largely built on neurotypical

models of motivation and reward. They assume a capacity for delayed gratification (challenging for DFR and PUR), consistent attention (difficult for IMA), and linear planning (hard for VTO). This creates an "incentive trap" where DDD individuals are inherently disadvantaged. Long-term goals feel unmotivating, bureaucratic processes are insurmountable, and access to crucial support (like diagnosis and specialized care) is often restricted by complex, time-consuming hurdles.

9. Neurochemical Hijacking (Chapter 13):
10. Perhaps the most alarming external pressure is the deliberate or unwitting exploitation of our neurobiological vulnerabilities by modern industries. Social media, gaming, ultra-processed foods, and instant entertainment platforms are meticulously designed to deliver rapid, variable dopamine "hits," directly targeting our PUR and DFR. This "neurochemical hijacking" creates addictive loops, fragments our attention (IMA), and fosters an insatiable craving for instant gratification, making engagement with the real world's slower, more nuanced rewards feel dull by comparison. This is a powerful, pervasive force that actively works against our well-being.

These external burdens are not abstract concepts; they are tangible forces that shape the daily lives of DDD individuals, often leading to chronic stress, underachievement, and profound emotional distress. Recognizing them is the first step towards dismantling them.

## *The Path to Empowerment: Strategies for Bridging the Gap*

Despite the profound challenges, this book is ultimately a testament to the immense potential for empowerment and flourishing. We have outlined a multi-faceted approach to bridging the reality gap, integrating internal mastery with external advocacy.

1. Radical Self-Acceptance and Intentional Self-Care (Chapter 1):
2. The foundation of well-being lies in embracing your neurodivergent identity. This means moving beyond shame and self-blame, cultivating self-compassion, and prioritizing self-care that is specifically tailored to the needs of your DDD brain. This includes structured routines, mindful movement, nourishing nutrition, and adequate sleep – all designed to support your unique neurobiology.
3. Multimodal Treatment and the Power of Informed Choice (Chapter 2 & 11):
4. Effective management of DDD often requires a combination of strategies. We demystified the pharmacological landscape, explaining how medications can act as crucial tools to normalize dopamine levels, much like insulin for diabetes. When used appropriately, medication can provide the neurochemical foundation necessary for other interventions to be truly effective. Beyond medication, psychotherapy (like CBT, DBT), specialized coaching, and educational support are vital for developing coping skills, processing emotional experiences, and

building executive function strategies. Making informed choices about your treatment plan, in collaboration with neuro-affirmative professionals, is a powerful act of self-advocacy.

5. Emotional Self-Regulation and Mastery (Chapter 4 & 6):
6. Learning to navigate your intense emotional symphony is key. We explored strategies for:

- **Recognizing and Validating Emotions:** Using tools like journaling and mood trackers to understand your internal landscape and counter the sting of **RSD**.
- **Expressing Emotions Authentically:** Leveraging creative outlets and assertive communication techniques to convey your feelings effectively.
- **Regulating Emotions:** Employing DDD-specific strategies like short, engaging breathing exercises, targeted physical activity (DRC activation), and sensory grounding techniques to manage **ARA** and prevent overwhelm.
- **Transforming Emotions:** Utilizing cognitive reframing and structured problem-solving to rewire negative thought patterns and turn challenges into growth opportunities.
- **Healing Emotional Children:** Addressing past wounds and internalizing self-compassion to resolve deep-seated emotional patterns.
- **Becoming the Emotional Adult:** Cultivating self-differentiation and emotional intelligence to navigate relationships and challenges with greater autonomy and wisdom.

1. Conscious Social Navigation and Authentic Connection

(Chapter 7 & 8):

2. We provided practical tools for navigating the neurotypical social world, understanding how your DDD traits might be misinterpreted, and adapting your approach without sacrificing authenticity. This includes strategies for:

- **Avoiding Unintentional Blunders:** Proactive planning and self-monitoring to mitigate misinterpretations stemming from **IMA, PUR, VTO, and TAMD.**
- **Decoding Neurotypical Communication:** Recognizing invalidating phrases and responding in ways that protect your emotional sovereignty and reinforce your boundaries.
- **Cultivating Connectedness:** Prioritizing quality over quantity in relationships, seeking neuro-affirming spaces, and practicing authentic unmasking to build genuine belonging.

1. Authentic Networking and Community Building (Chapter 9 & 14):
2. Networking, when approached through a neuro-affirmative lens, becomes a powerful tool for finding your "tribe." We explored strategies for:

- **Seeking Your People:** Leveraging online communities and aligned events to connect with individuals who share your interests and values.
- **Being Ready:** Strategic preparation, setting realistic goals, and crafting authentic pitches to navigate social interactions with confidence.

- **Being Yourself:** Embracing your DDD identity as a strength, understanding the cost of masking, and strategically disclosing your neurodivergence to foster deeper, more sustainable connections.
- **Building Community:** Recognizing the profound power of collective support, shared experiences, and mutual validation in reducing isolation and fostering resilience.

1. Leveraging Strengths for Entrepreneurship (Chapter 3):
2. We specifically highlighted how the very traits of DDD—creativity, hyperfocus, resilience, curiosity, and risk-taking—are not just compatible with entrepreneurship but can be powerful advantages. We provided strategies for harnessing these strengths while managing common pitfalls like procrastination and disorganization, demonstrating that your DDD can be a blueprint for innovation and impact.

## *The Continuum Dopaminergique: A Vision for Neuro-Inclusion*

Underpinning all these strategies is the revolutionary concept of the **"Continuum Dopaminergique" (Chapter 12)**. This perspective shifts us away from a binary "ADHD/no ADHD" diagnosis to a nuanced understanding of human neurobiological diversity. It recognizes that variations in dopaminergic functioning exist across the entire population, with DDD representing one end of this spectrum where these variations lead to significant functional impairment.

This continuum fosters:

- **Greater Empathy:** By understanding that everyone's brain operates on a spectrum, it cultivates compassion for diverse ways of thinking, feeling, and behaving.
- **Personalized Approaches:** It validates that there is no "one-size-fits-all" solution, encouraging tailored interventions that respect an individual's unique position on the spectrum.
- **Celebration of Strengths:** It highlights that even at the "DDD" end of the spectrum, there are inherent strengths and unique perspectives that enrich society.

This vision of a neuro-inclusive future is one where neurological differences are not merely tolerated but genuinely recognized, respected, and celebrated as a natural and valuable component of human diversity. It is a future where educational systems, workplaces, healthcare models, and societal norms are consciously designed to accommodate a wide range of neurotypes, dismantling the "incentive traps" and mitigating the "neurochemical hijacking" that currently disadvantage so many.

## A Call to Action: Your Role in Shaping the Future

This book is more than a collection of insights; it is a call to action. The journey toward a neuro-inclusive future requires collective effort, beginning with each of us.

- **Embrace Your Identity:** If you are a neurodivergent individual, embrace your unique brain. Understand its wiring, celebrate its strengths, and learn to navigate its challenges with self-compassion and effective strategies. Your authenticity is your power.
- **Advocate for Yourself:** Become an informed patient, a proactive employee, a self-aware partner. Communicate your needs clearly, set healthy boundaries, and seek the support you deserve. Your personal advocacy is a powerful ripple effect.
- **Build Your Community:** Seek out and connect with others who understand your experience. The validation, shared wisdom, and collective strength of community are invaluable resources in a world that can feel isolating.
- **Educate and Advocate for Others:** Share your knowledge. Challenge misinformation and stigma wherever you encounter it. Speak out for policy changes that promote neuro-inclusive education, workplaces, and healthcare. Engage with organizations dedicated to neurodiversity advocacy. Remember, a more inclusive society for neuro-divergents is a better society for everyone.
- **Neurotypical Allies:** If you are neurotypical, your role is crucial. Listen with an open mind, learn with genuine curiosity, and use your privilege to amplify neurodivergent voices and dismantle systemic barriers. Your empathy and active support are invaluable.

The chapters of this book have provided a map, a compass, and a lexicon. But the most important chapters are yet to be written – by you. Your personal journey of self-discovery, your acts of courage in self-advocacy, and your contributions to building a more understanding world will shape the future.

This is not a definitive answer or a magic formula. It is a memoir, a reflection, and a celebration. It is a work in progress, a work of art, and above all, a work of love.

**Remember:** You are not broken. You are not defective. You are uniquely wired, and that is your strength.

Let your journey continue, armed with knowledge, fueled by self-compassion, and guided by the vision of a world where every brain is valued, every voice is heard, and every individual can truly bridge the reality gap to live a fulfilling and meaningful life.

**Further Reading and Resources:**

For those interested in deepening their understanding and continuing their journey, here are some invaluable resources:

- **ADHD Entrepreneur:** A dedicated website offering information, resources, and coaching specifically tailored for entrepreneurs with ADHD, helping them leverage their unique strengths.
- **The Power of Neurodiversity:** A compelling TED Talk by Dr. Thomas Armstrong, which eloquently explains how neurodiversity is a profound source of innovation and creativity, challenging conventional views.
- **Driven to Distraction at Work:** A practical and insightful book by Dr. Edward Hallowell, offering actionable solutions and strategies for managing ADHD effectively in the workplace.
- **The Dyslexic Advantage:** A groundbreaking book by Drs. Brock and Fernette Eide, revealing how the unique cognitive patterns associated with dyslexia can be a significant advantage in diverse fields such as business, science,

art, and education.

- **The Gift of Adult ADD:** A transformative book by Dr. Lara Honos-Webb, which provides guidance on how to reframe the challenges of ADHD into gifts of creativity, enthusiasm, and hyperfocus, empowering individuals to thrive.
- **ADHD Awareness Month:** An essential online hub providing up-to-date information, resources, and event listings related to ADHD awareness and advocacy efforts globally.
- **ADHD Stigma: The Power of Words:** A powerful video resource that highlights the critical impact of language on perceptions and treatment of individuals with ADHD, advocating for more compassionate and accurate terminology.
- **ADHD Voices:** A website featuring a collection of personal stories and videos from individuals with ADHD, offering diverse perspectives and lived experiences.
- **Attention Deficit Disorder Association (ADDA):** A leading organization providing comprehensive support, education, and advocacy specifically for adults with ADHD.
- **Children and Adults with Attention-Deficit/Hyperactivity Disorder (CHADD):** A national resource offering extensive information, support, and services for individuals with ADHD and their families across all age groups.
- **How to Be an Ally to Someone with ADHD:** An insightful article providing practical tips and advice for friends, partners, and colleagues on how to be genuinely supportive of someone with ADHD.

- **Stigma Experienced by Adults with Attention-Deficit/Hyperactivity Disorder: A Systematic Review:** A rigorous scientific paper that synthesizes research on the sources, types, effects, and coping strategies related to stigma experienced by adults with ADHD.

# Epilogue

## The Unfolding Manifesto: Embodying DDD and Co-Creating a Neuro-Inclusive Future

**Introduction: The Genesis of a New Understanding**

This book has been more than a mere exploration; it has been an invitation to a new way of seeing, understanding, and embracing the neurodivergent experience. We embarked on this journey with a fundamental premise: that the traditional narrative surrounding "ADHD" was incomplete, often misleading, and deeply stigmatizing. Our purpose has been to challenge the incoherent and often pathologizing framing of Attention Deficit Hyperactivity Disorder, replacing it with a more precise, neurobiologically grounded, and ultimately empowering concept: **Dopamine Deficit Disorder (DDD)**. We have sought to illuminate the invisible emergency that shapes the lives of millions, transforming perceived "flaws" into understandable manifestations of a distinct neurochemical architecture.

Throughout these pages, we have peeled back the layers of misunderstanding, revealing the profound impact of DDD on every facet of existence – from the nuanced challenges of executive function to the often-misinterpreted intensity of emotional experiences. We have confronted the pervasive weight of **stigma and discrimination**, exposing how societal ignorance and systemic biases amplify the inherent difficulties, creating unnecessary suffering and limiting boundless potential. Yet, our journey has been equally dedicated to unveiling the extraordinary strengths woven into the fabric of the DDD brain: the unparalleled creativity, the laser-like focus, the audacious spirit of innovation, and the profound empathy that define so many with this neurotype. We have offered practical strategies, not as a means to "fix" who you are, but to empower you to navigate a world that is still catching up to the breadth of human neurodiversity.

This Epilogue is not an endpoint, but a launching pad. It is a synthesis of our collective insights, a reaffirmation of the DDD paradigm, and a fervent call to action. It invites you, whether you identify as DDD, as a neurotypical ally, or as simply curious, to join us in co-creating a future where understanding triumphs over ignorance, where diversity is celebrated as a strength, and where every mind, in its unique brilliance, can flourish without apology.

**Reclaiming the Narrative: The Power of Naming DDD**

The most significant shift this book advocates for is the re-naming of ADHD to **Dopamine Deficit Disorder (DDD)**. This is not a superficial semantic exercise; it is a profound reorientation, a reclamation of narrative that holds immense power for self-understanding, medical clarity, and societal acceptance.

The term "ADHD" has long been a source of profound inadequacy and harm. It is inherently incoherent, focusing on a single symptom (attention deficit) while failing to capture the full spectrum of the condition. "Hyperactivity" is often absent in adult presentations or manifests internally, making the label a poor fit for many. More critically, the term places the emphasis on a *deficit* within the individual's "attention," fostering a pervasive sense of brokenness, inadequacy, and blame. It implies a moral failing—a lack of effort or willpower—rather than a neurobiological reality. This linguistic framing contributes directly to internalized shame and fuels the external stigma that has plagued generations. How many times have individuals with "ADHD" heard, "Just try harder," or "You're just lazy," echoing the very inaccuracies embedded in the name?

**DDD**, by contrast, is precise, medical, and empowering. It immediately centers the discussion on the core neurochemical dysregulation: an atypical functioning of the dopaminergic system. This is the **"invisible emergency"** we have explored throughout this book – a brain that constantly seeks dopamine to regulate attention, motivation, and emotion, often leading to a **Phenotype of Urgency for Reward (PUR)** and a relentless **Drive for Novelty and Risk (DFR)**. By naming the underlying mechanism, we achieve several critical shifts:

1. **Scientific Accuracy:** It aligns with contemporary neuroscientific understanding, moving beyond symptom description to root cause. This opens doors for more targeted research and the development of more effective, compassionate interventions.

2. **Reduced Self-Blame and Stigma:** When you understand that your struggles with **Volition and Task Organization (VTO)**, **Inattention Modulation Instability (IMA)**, or **Affective Reactivity Amplification (ARA)** stem from a neurochemical difference, the shame dis-

solves. It's not a moral failing; it's a difference in brain wiring. This shift in perspective is foundational for radical self-acceptance.

3. **Empowered Communication:** The new lexicon—PUR, IMA, DFR, ARA, VTO, TAMD, DRC—provides individuals with a powerful toolkit to articulate their internal experience with clarity and precision. Instead of vaguely saying, "I get distracted," you can explain, "My **Inattention Modulation Instability (IMA)** makes it hard to filter irrelevant stimuli, so I need a quiet environment to focus." This elevates the conversation from subjective complaint to objective neurobiological reality, fostering greater understanding from others and enabling more effective self-advocacy.

4. **Targeted Solutions:** By understanding the underlying dopamine dysregulation, interventions—whether pharmacological, therapeutic, or behavioral—can be more precisely tailored to support the **Dopaminergic Reward Circuit (DRC)**, manage urgency (PUR), and enhance executive function (VTO). It shifts the focus from symptom suppression to neurochemical optimization and support.

Embracing DDD means reclaiming agency over one's narrative. It allows individuals to see themselves not as "disordered" but as part of a distinct neurotype, navigating a world that has, until now, failed to recognize their unique operating system. This name change is foundational to bridging the reality gap, both internally and externally.

### Bridging the Reality Gap: An Intersectional Effort

The "reality gap" is the chasm that exists between the internal experience of a DDD individual and the external expectations and structures of a neurotypical-centric world. Bridging this gap is the central challenge and the ultimate aspiration of this manifesto. It requires a multi-pronged approach, demanding effort from both the individual and society at large.

**The Internal Gap: Mastery and Self-Acceptance**

For the individual with DDD, bridging the internal gap is a journey of profound self-discovery and mastery. It involves:

1. **Understanding Your Unique Neurotype:** Moving beyond a superficial diagnosis to truly comprehend how your **PUR, IMA, DFR, ARA, VTO, TAMD, and DRC** shape your thoughts, emotions, and behaviors. This knowledge is the bedrock of self-compassion.

2. **Radical Self-Acceptance:** Embracing your neurodivergence not as a flaw to be fixed, but as an integral part of your identity. This involves shedding internalized shame, challenging self-blame, and celebrating your unique strengths. It is the courageous act of being authentically yourself, even when it feels counter-cultural.

3. **Cultivating Emotional Self-Regulation:** Developing personalized strategies to navigate the intensity of **Affective Reactivity Amplification (ARA)** and the sting of **Rejection Sensitive Dysphoria (RSD)**. This includes mindful practices, emotional literacy, and building a toolkit of coping mechanisms that support your neurobiology.

4. **Strategic Self-Management:** Implementing concrete, DDD-friendly strategies for executive function challenges (VTO). This might involve external scaffolding (timers,

visual aids), energy budgeting for social interactions (IMA), or leveraging hyperfocus for deep work.

5. **Authentic Communication:** Learning to articulate your needs and experiences clearly and assertively, breaking the cycle of misunderstanding and fostering genuine connection. This involves both expressing your internal reality and understanding neurotypical communication styles.

These internal strategies are not about conforming; they are about empowering you to thrive within your own neurobiological framework, reducing friction and cultivating inner peace.

## The External Gap: Challenging the Status Quo

The individual journey, however, is insufficient if the external world remains unyielding and unaccommodating. Bridging the external gap requires systemic change, challenging the deeply ingrained assumptions and structures built on neurotypical norms. This involves:

1. **Dismantling Stigma and Discrimination:** Through education, advocacy, and direct confrontation of harmful stereotypes, we must dismantle the societal prejudices that limit opportunities and foster shame. This includes advocating for respectful language, accurate media representation, and legal protections against discrimination.
2. **Redesigning Systems for Neuro-Inclusion:** Our educational institutions, workplaces, healthcare systems, and even urban planning are often inadvertently hostile to

neurodivergent individuals. We must advocate for:

- **Flexible Workplaces:** Embracing diverse work styles, offering flexible hours, quiet zones, and sensory-friendly environments.
- **Inclusive Education:** Tailoring learning environments to accommodate diverse cognitive styles, moving beyond standardized testing that disadvantages neurodivergent students.
- **Accessible Healthcare:** Ensuring that diagnostic processes are timely, affordable, and neuro-affirmative, and that treatment options are comprehensive and culturally competent.
- **Challenging the Incentive Trap:** Re-evaluating societal reward systems to ensure they do not inherently disadvantage brains that struggle with delayed gratification (PUR) or sustained motivation on uninteresting tasks (DFR).
- **Combating Neurochemical Hijacking:** Raising awareness about how modern digital environments exploit DDD vulnerabilities and advocating for ethical design principles that promote well-being over addiction.

## The Two-Way Bridge: Mutual Understanding and Empathy

Ultimately, bridging the reality gap is a two-way street. It requires neurodivergent individuals to understand the neurotypical world, and neurotypical individuals to understand the neurodivergent world. It is a dialogue, not a demand.

- **For Neurodivergent Individuals:** Your role is to educate, advocate, and articulate your needs with clarity and self-compassion. It is also to extend empathy, recognizing that neurotypical individuals may genuinely lack understanding.
- **For Neurotypical Individuals:** Your role is to listen with an open mind, learn without judgment, challenge your own biases, and actively create spaces of genuine inclusion. It means moving beyond mere tolerance to true appreciation of neurodiversity as a valuable aspect of human variation.

This mutual effort is the essence of a truly neuro-inclusive society.

**The Manifesto Unfolds: Embodying DDD Strengths**

The true power of this book lies in its unwavering focus on strengths. DDD is not a deficit to be overcome, but a distinct way of being that harbors immense potential, particularly in a world craving innovation and authentic connection.

The "disorder" in Dopamine Deficit Disorder refers to a *dysregulation* of a vital system, not a broken human being. Within this unique wiring lie profound strengths that are not merely compensatory mechanisms, but genuine advantages:

- **Unleashed Creativity and Innovation:** The divergent thinking, the ability to make novel connections across seemingly unrelated ideas, and the inherent **Drive for Novelty and Risk (DFR)** fuel a wellspring of original thought. DDD brains are often pioneers, generating solutions others simply don't conceive.
- **Hyperfocus as a Superpower:** When a task ignites

interest, the **Inattention Modulation Instability (IMA)** transforms into an extraordinary capacity for deep, sustained focus. This allows for rapid mastery, intense productivity, and profound immersion in passion projects, turning ideas into reality with unparalleled speed.

- **Resilience Forged in Fire:** A lifetime of navigating a world that often misunderstood or punished their neurotype cultivates immense resilience. DDD individuals often possess an incredible ability to bounce back from setbacks, pivot rapidly, and find innovative paths forward where others might give up.
- **Profound Empathy and Intuition (ARA):** While challenging, the heightened emotional reactivity of **Affective Reactivity Amplification (ARA)** can also lead to deep empathy, allowing for intuitive understanding of others' emotional states. This fosters authentic connection and can be a powerful asset in leadership and interpersonal dynamics.
- **Entrepreneurial Drive and Audacity:** The comfort with risk (DFR), the urgent need for action (PUR), the ability to think outside the box, and the capacity for intense passion make DDD individuals natural entrepreneurs. They are often less bound by conventional wisdom, more willing to take leaps of faith, and possess an unwavering dedication to their vision.
- **Authenticity and Directness:** When unmasked and in safe spaces, DDD individuals often exude a genuine, unfiltered authenticity that cuts through superficiality, fostering deeper and more meaningful connections.

Embodying DDD means embracing these strengths, not as

isolated talents, but as interconnected facets of a powerful neurotype. It means consciously seeking environments, careers, and relationships where these strengths are not just tolerated, but actively celebrated and leveraged. This is the journey from coping to flourishing, from managing deficits to maximizing potential.

**The Call to Action: Architecting a Neuro-Inclusive Future**

Our journey together culminates in a resounding call to action, a collective commitment to build a future where neurodiversity is not just acknowledged but truly integrated and valued. This is a multi-layered endeavor, requiring individual courage, communal solidarity, and systemic transformation.

**Individual Empowerment: A Lifelong Journey**

Your journey of self-discovery, self-acceptance, and self-empowerment is ongoing. It is a daily practice of:

- **Continuous Learning:** Stay curious about your own neurotype. Explore new research, engage with neurodivergent thought leaders, and continually refine your understanding of how your brain works.
- **Radical Self-Compassion:** Treat yourself with the same kindness and understanding you would offer a loved one. Recognize that your challenges are not moral failings but neurological realities. Forgive yourself for past missteps and celebrate every small victory.
- **Sustained Self-Care:** Prioritize well-being that is tailored to your DDD needs. This includes consistent routines, sensory regulation, adequate rest, nourishing food, and

movement that activates your **Dopaminergic Reward Circuit (DRC)**. Recognize that self-care is not selfish; it is foundational for your capacity to thrive.

- **Strategic Self-Advocacy:** Learn to articulate your needs and boundaries clearly and respectfully. This involves asking for accommodations at work or school, communicating your communication style to loved ones, and seeking out neuro-affirmative professionals who truly understand DDD.

## Community as Sanctuary and Catalyst

No one can bridge the reality gap alone. The power of collective identity and shared experience is immense.

- **Seek Your Tribe:** Actively cultivate relationships with other neurodivergent individuals who understand your struggles and celebrate your strengths. These communities provide invaluable validation, practical advice, and a sense of belonging that combats isolation and **Rejection Sensitive Dysphoria (RSD)**.
- **Offer Mutual Support:** Contribute to these communities. Share your experiences, offer encouragement, and lend your unique insights. The act of supporting others reinforces your own strength and purpose.
- **Collective Identity:** Recognize that by connecting with others, you become part of a larger movement. This collective identity fuels advocacy and provides a powerful antidote to feeling "othered."

## Systemic Transformation: Challenging the Status Quo

The ultimate goal is to reshape the very structures of society to be neuro-inclusive. This requires persistent, multifaceted advocacy:

- **Education Reform:** Advocating for educational systems that embrace diverse learning styles, offer personalized support, move beyond rigid curricula, and understand DDD not as a deficit, but as a different way of learning. This includes training educators in neurodiversity-affirming practices.
- **Workplace Evolution:** Pushing for workplaces that prioritize neuro-inclusion through flexible schedules, sensory-friendly environments, clear communication protocols, diverse hiring practices, and leadership that values neurodivergent contributions. This means moving beyond tokenism to genuine integration.
- **Healthcare Advancement:** Demanding accessible, affordable, and neuro-affirmative diagnostic and treatment pathways for DDD. This includes advocating for expanded insurance coverage, specialized training for medical professionals, and a holistic approach that considers mental, emotional, and physical well-being.
- **Legal and Policy Advocacy:** Working to ensure that anti-discrimination laws protect neurodivergent individuals and that policies are developed with neuro-inclusive principles at their core.
- **Media Representation:** Challenging harmful stereotypes and advocating for accurate, nuanced, and positive portrayals of neurodivergent individuals in media, entertain-

ment, and public discourse. This helps dismantle stigma at its root.

## The Role of Neurotypical Allies: Active Partners in Progress

For our neurotypical allies, your partnership is invaluable.

- **Listen and Learn:** Approach neurodivergent experiences with genuine curiosity and a willingness to learn. Listen to lived experiences, consume neurodivergent-authored content, and challenge your own ingrained biases.
- **Amplify Voices:** Use your privilege and platform to amplify neurodivergent voices, perspectives, and demands.
- **Create Inclusive Environments:** Consciously design and advocate for spaces—physical, social, and professional—that are welcoming and accommodating to diverse neurotypes. Ask, "How can this be more accessible for different brains?"
- **Challenge Misinformation:** Speak up against stigma, stereotypes, and ableism whenever you encounter them. Be an active advocate for understanding and acceptance.

## Our Collective Journey: Beyond the Epilogue

This book, this manifesto, is a culmination of shared insights, lived experiences, and a fervent hope for a future defined by understanding and acceptance. It is a testament to the resilience, creativity, and profound contributions of neurodivergent individuals.

We believe, with unwavering conviction, that neurodivergent adults have an extraordinary amount to offer society. We believe that, when supported and understood, neurodivergent individuals can achieve profound success, experience deep happiness, and lead immensely fulfilling lives. We believe that the **"reality gap"** is not an insurmountable chasm, but a bridge waiting to be built—a bridge of empathy, knowledge, and collective action.

We are proud to be neurodivergent. We are proud to embody the unique strengths of DDD. We are proud to be ourselves, without apology or reservation.

We invite you, wholeheartedly, to join us in this ongoing journey. A journey of radical self-discovery, unwavering self-acceptance, and boundless self-empowerment. We invite you to be a part of the movement to truly bridge the reality gap – to champion the new understanding of **Dopamine Deficit Disorder (DDD)**, to celebrate the rich tapestry of neurodiversity, and to co-create a world where every brain is not just tolerated, but celebrated as an indispensable component of human flourishing. The future, with all its innovation, empathy, and authentic connection, awaits.

# Afterword

The Echo of Urgency, the Resonance of Identity –
Continuing the LexiNeuroHub Journey

We have reached the concluding pages of this book, but truly,
we stand at the threshold of a new beginning – the continuation
of a journey we now share. We sincerely hope that this
exploration has resonated deeply with you, that it has ignited
new understanding, and imparted invaluable insights into the
multifaceted landscape of the neurodivergent experience. Our
core aspiration was to illuminate how what has long been
mislabeled as "ADHD" is, in fact, **Dopamine Deficit Disorder
(DDD)** – a profound source of both unique challenges and
extraordinary strengths, particularly within the dynamic realm
of entrepreneurship.

Through these chapters, we have dared to challenge pre-
vailing narratives, to dissect the very essence of DDD, and to
offer a revolutionary lexicon that empowers you to articulate
your internal world with unprecedented clarity. We have
moved beyond the vague and often stigmatizing "incoherence
of ADHD," a term that has historically contributed to self-
blame and external misunderstanding. By focusing on the

neurochemical reality—the "invisible emergency" of dopamine dysregulation—we aimed to provide a foundation for true self-compassion. This shift in understanding means that your experiences with **Phenotype of Urgency for Reward (PUR), Inattention Modulation Instability (IMA), Drive for Novelty and Risk (DFR), Affective Reactivity Amplification (ARA), Volition and Task Organization (VTO),** and **Delayed Access to Dynamic Memory (TAMD)** are no longer viewed as personal failings, but as direct manifestations of your unique **Dopaminergic Reward Circuit (DRC).** This precise language, we believe, is a powerful tool for bridging the internal reality gap – transforming confusion into clarity, and self-criticism into self-acceptance.

We hope you have found not just knowledge, but profound inspiration and practical guidance within these pages. The stories and examples of entrepreneurs who have leveraged their DDD as a hidden advantage are not mere anecdotes; they are blueprints for possibility, living proof that the very traits often misunderstood can propel you towards remarkable achievement and meaningful impact. Your divergent thinking, your capacity for hyperfocus, your inherent creativity, and your resilience are not limitations; they are entrepreneurial superpowers awaiting activation. This book has endeavored to show you how to harness these strengths, to navigate the potential pitfalls, and to forge a path that is uniquely yours.

Beyond the intellectual insights, it is our deepest hope that you have also experienced a powerful sense of connection and belonging with us, and with the vast, vibrant community of other neurodivergent adults who share your struggles, your triumphs, and your audacious aspirations. In a world that often demands conformity, it is vital to know that you are unequivocally not alone. You are not defective; you are precisely and wonderfully unique. You are not hopeless; you are powerful, resilient, and brimming with potential. This shared realization is the genesis of true liberation.

We extend our heartfelt gratitude for your unwavering time and attention, for the curiosity that led you to these pages, and for the invaluable feedback and support we have received. Your presence and participation have enriched this endeavor immeasurably, and we deeply value your opinions and suggestions as we continually strive to improve and expand this crucial conversation.

As the authors and architects of this journey, we now extend a personal invitation: an invitation to remain connected, to deepen your understanding, and to actively join our expanding global community—the **LexiNeuroHub family**.

**LexiNeuroHub** is more than just a name; it is an evolution of our shared mission, a dynamic ecosystem dedicated to empowering neurodivergent individuals and fostering a truly inclusive world. It is built upon the very principles explored in this book: understanding the neurochemical basis of DDD, celebrating neurodivergent strengths, providing practical strategies, and advocating for systemic change.

We invite you to visit our website, tdahfrance.com, to explore our mission, vision, and values, and to discover the wealth of resources available. This hub is designed to be your compass for navigating the complexities of DDD, offering a curated space for ongoing learning, growth, and connection.

We also encourage you to follow us on our various social media platforms, including [Facebook], [Twitter], [Instagram], [LinkedIn], and [YouTube]. Here, you will receive real-time updates on the latest news, upcoming events, and groundbreaking activities within the DDD community. Engage in discussions, share your own insights, and find daily inspiration from a network that truly understands.

To further enrich your journey, we invite you to subscribe to our newsletter and podcast. These platforms are designed to deliver in-depth insights, actionable tips, and expert advice directly to you, empowering you to thrive as a neurodivergent individual and entrepreneur. Our content will continue to delve into the nuances of DDD, offering practical strategies for managing challenges, harnessing strengths, and navigating the professional and personal landscapes with authenticity and purpose.

Most importantly, we want to reiterate a core message of this book: **Take action and pursue your entrepreneurial dreams.** You possess an extraordinary toolkit of inherent strengths. You have **Dopamine Deficit Disorder**, and that, as we've demonstrated, is not a disadvantage but a profound and often hidden advantage. Do not allow past narratives, societal misconceptions, or internalized doubts to diminish your vision. You have the creativity, the resilience, the passion, and the unique perspective to innovate, to lead, and to make an indelible mark on the world. Your brain, with its distinct wiring, is precisely what the world needs to solve complex problems and envision a brighter future.

We are here, as founders, as advocates, and as fellow travelers, to support you every step of the way. We will cheer for your triumphs, offer guidance through your challenges, and celebrate every milestone on your path.

We are immensely proud to be neurodivergent. We are immensely proud to be entrepreneurs, leveraging our unique neurotype to build and innovate. And we are profoundly proud to be part of the **LexiNeuroHub family**, a growing movement dedicated to understanding, empowerment, and authentic connection.

Thank you for embarking on this transformative journey with us. We look forward to continuing this vital conversation and building a neuro-inclusive future, together, as part of the LexiNeuroHub family.

With gratitude and anticipation,

Paul Cambria

Founder and CEO of TDAH France: Comprendre & Agir

TDAH France: Comprendre & Agir website: http://www.td ahfrance.com

# About the Author

Paul Cambria is a visionary neurodivergent entrepreneur, accomplished author, and sought-after speaker, dedicated to empowering the neurodivergent community. He is the founder and CEO of **TDAH France: Comprendre & Agir**, a non-profit organization at the forefront of developing innovative technology and solutions for individuals with neurodiversity.

A leading voice in the field, Paul is the acclaimed author of several pivotal works on Dopamine Deficit Disorder (DDD) and entrepreneurship, including:

*Dopamine Deficit Disorder: A Manifesto of Urgency & Identity*
*Bridging the Reality Gap*
*The Neurodivergent Advantage*
*How to Thrive as a Neurodivergent Entrepreneur*

His insights are frequently featured across various media platforms, from podcasts and blogs to magazines. Paul's profound passion lies in raising awareness and fostering understanding of neurodiversity, relentlessly advocating for and empowering neurodivergent adults to achieve their fullest personal and professional potential.

He currently resides in the picturesque region of Tuscany, Italy, where he is a devoted father of four children.

To learn more about Paul Cambria and his transformative work, please visit his website or connect with him on LinkedIn, Twitter, or Facebook.

**You can connect with me on:**

- http://www.tdahfrance.com
- https://x.com/ADHDConnect1
- https://www.facebook.com/LexiNeuroHub
- https://www.linkedin.com/in/adhd-connect

www.ingramcontent.com/pod-product-compliance
Lightning Source LLC
Chambersburg PA
CBHW050908260726
48660CB00001B/99